Jesus Two Thousand Years Later

FAITH AND SCHOLARSHIP
COLLOQUIES SERIES

What Has Archaeology to Do with Faith?
The Old and New Testaments
Images of Jesus Today
Earthing Christologies
The Dead Sea Scrolls and Christian Faith
Jesus Two Thousand Years Later

Jesus Two Thousand Years Later

Edited by
James H. Charlesworth
and Walter P. Weaver

Faith and Scholarship Colloquies

Trinity Press International   Harrisburg, Pa.

Copyright © 2000 by Trinity Press International

Trinity Press International, P.O. Box 1321, Harrisburg, PA 17105
Trinity Press International is a division of the Morehouse Group.

Cover art: The Savior, Andrei Rublev (1360–c. 1430).
Tretyakov Gallery, Moscow, Russia. Scala/Art Resource, New York.

Cover design: Jim Booth

Library of Congress Cataloging-in-Publication Data
Jesus two thousand years later / edited by James H. Charlesworth and
Walter P. Weaver.
    p. cm. — (Faith and scholarship colloquies)
    Includes bibliographical references and index.
    ISBN 1-56338-303-9
    1. Jesus Christ – Historicity. 2. Jesus Christ – Biography – History and
criticism. I. Charlesworth, James H. II. Weaver, Walter P. III. Series.
BT303.2.J47 1999
232.9'08 – dc21   99-053669

Printed in the United States of America

00 01 02 03 04 05 06   10 9 8 7 6 5 4 3 2 1

For Frances DeMott,
whose kindness keeps alive
this series of colloquies
for present and future generations

Contents

Contributors

JAMES H. CHARLESWORTH is George L. Collord Professor of New Testament Language and Literature at Princeton Theological Seminary and Director of the Seminary's Dead Sea Scrolls project.

JOHN DOMINIC CROSSAN is Professor Emeritus of Religious Studies at DePaul University.

AMY-JILL LEVINE is E. Rhodes and Leona B. Carpenter Professor of New Testament Studies, Vanderbilt Divinity School, Vanderbilt University.

E. P. SANDERS is Arts and Sciences Professor of Religion at Duke University.

WALTER P. WEAVER is the Pendergrass Professor, Emeritus, at Florida Southern College.

Series Description

Faith and Scholarship Colloquies

This series explores the boundaries where faith and academic study intersect. At these borders, the sharp edge of current biblical scholarship is allowed to cut theologically and pose its often challenging questions for traditional faith. The series includes contributions from leading scholars in contemporary biblical studies. As Christian faith seeks to send a word on target in our day, as powerful as those in the past, it needs to sharpen its perception and proclamation from honest and truthful insights in human knowledge, from first-century archaeology to modern linguistics.

Introduction

The question that Jesus was said to have addressed to his disciples, in a renowned scene (Mark 8:27ff.), still lingers today, "Who do people say that I am?" And the multiplicity of answers continues unabated, from the more traditional confession, "You are the Christ" (or, appealing to the Matthean elaboration, "The Christ, the Son of the living God"), to the more learned opinions of the experts. In fact, scholars have added other options across the years: the apocalyptic visionary, the prophet, the social reformer, the Cynic peasant leader of an egalitarian movement, the political agitator, the rabbinic teacher of an idealistic ethic. Was he in fact none of these or all of these? or something different yet to be proposed? The latter seems unlikely; the possibilities are clearly limited. The usual churchgoing believer is more often unaware of these variations; for him or her the only Jesus is the one handed down through the faith community and loosely based on the picture(s) elaborated in the New Testament. That there might be a difference between the historical reality of Jesus and the faith construal of him rarely occurs to this — admittedly hypothetical — believer.

We are today in a period of revived interest in what is broadly called the "historical Jesus." Whether the appropriate name to be given to this era is "third quest" or "Jesus research" depends on who is speaking; James Charlesworth prefers the

1

latter to describe an inquiry that is not driven by theological interest (see his essay in this volume), whereas the "quest of the historical Jesus" refers to a concern embracing questions of faith. The more characteristic terminology speaks of the "old quest," the "new quest," and now of a "third quest," though, in my judgment, that categorizing also slights some of the history, especially in non-German circles. (On this point, see my *The Historical Jesus in the Twentieth Century: 1900–1950* [Harrisburg, Pa.: Trinity Press International, 1999].) But whatever may be concluded concerning proper titles, there is no gainsaying the fact of the widespread interest in the subject matter. The days of form-critical silence are over; the darkness that hung over the whole question has been pierced, and new rays of light have emanated from scholarly circles more optimistic with regard to the sources and possessing further material made available archaeologically and methodologically. The disparity between our supposed ordinary believer and the critic has diminished somewhat, doubtless due to the pervasive impact of modern communications media, though nevertheless there remains something of an inability to participate on the part of the nonspecialist. To a degree, all disciplines share that dilemma; it is just not possible for those without the requisite training to become a full partner in the process. What that circumstance portends for the believer is a separate issue in itself that does not, however, interest everyone. Many simply enjoy the subject. And surely there is no compulsion to assume a faith stance in order also to become an investigator.

To lay hold of the fundamental problem, however, is not so simple. We might see it as an ancient conundrum, as presented by the early Church patriarch Tertullian, who once asked (probably through clenched teeth), "What has Athens to do with Jerusalem?" Tertullian was not known for his devotion to rationality (even though he was a trained lawyer), especially as that affected matters of faith. So Athens, with its symbolism of reason seeking truth, contrasts with Jerusalem, with its symbolism of faith seeking understanding, the dispassionate service of reason versus the prophetic call and critique. In truth, both came marching resolutely together into the Western consciousness, even if the tension has also at times been explosive. We are — reminiscent of Paul — debtor to both Jew and Greek, for better, for worse.

Fidelity to Athens has especially marked the modern era, with the Enlightenment ethic of a reason that knows few limits, that solves all problems and renders life manageable, if not subservient. And, indeed, where would we be without our cell phones, our televisions, our airplanes, or our electric current and medical science? We would be someplace where few would be willing to go anymore: back in the neverland of our struggling ancestors, of eking out an existence marked by poverty, social misery, and either a fatalism of suffering at the hands of an uncontrollable nature or a resignation born of eschatological submission. Even yet, of course, the benefits (perhaps qualifiable as "alleged") of science and technology have not been extended uniformly across the earth.

The same rationalism that spurred the Enlightenment also gave birth to the "historical Jesus." This particular Jesus was unknown before the Age of Reason brought him to light. Its desire to subject all authorities, ancient and modern, to the scrutiny of rational process led to the search for the human Jesus underlying all the centuries of faith confession to him. The results resembled those attending scholarly pursuit of other historical figures: widely varying, maybe even more so in this case, especially so where the sources available are themselves variable and subject to differing interpretations. It should not surprise, even if it still disturbs, that a stream of different Jesuses has appeared. At the same time, the variety should not be allowed to obscure many essential points of agreement.

The other side of Tertullian's disclaimer, Jerusalem, continues to infuse a distinctive element into the story. Christian faith, true to its Israelite — especially prophetic — heritage, has always bound itself to history. It speaks, not of timeless cycles of nature or the repetitions and rhythms of the natural order, but of unrepeatable historical events. Dates, places, sacred time and space, are all celebrated; to enter that particular faith community is not to vanish into the mystical beyond, but to stand in a world marked by particularity, living persons and deeds. Christian faith has always squished about in the muck of history and consequently cannot escape the ambiguity of all historical existence, even though some of its children — Fundamentalism, for example — have attempted to raise a barrier against the essential relativism of such existence. But an inerrant text — or, for that matter, an inerrant pope — cannot succeed in delivering faith from its fateful meeting with the facticity of its own foundations. Here Athens and Jerusalem converge, for good or evil. So seen from Athens, the quest looks like another venture of human reason as it probes and interrogates its own past; seen from Jerusalem, it looks like faith raking up its own prophetic inheritance in the name of faithfulness to its historical roots.

We cannot go with Tertullian down some schizophrenic road, dividing reason and faith. Luther to the contrary, these two are like Jesus and John the Baptist, forever linked in a relationship that can be symbiotic, can be fatal, but is always tension filled. In this sense the historical Jesus is part of our past as well as our modern destiny and cannot be disowned without disowning ourselves.

The volume presented here offers the reader some samples of journeys down that road whose twin branches pass through Athens and Jerusalem. The guides are major figures themselves in the current resurgence of interest in the question of the historical Jesus. Here various eminent scholars provide their knowledge of the ways to enter the problem along with some specific instances of issues in the study of the historical Jesus. John Dominic Crossan takes us into the debate that the project of the historical Jesus provokes within the community of faith and proposes some distinctive responses out of his own wide-ranging experience of the current discussion. E. P. Sanders sets forth with expert lucidity how scholars determine what elements can legitimately be said to belong to the historical Jesus. From the Jewish side, Amy-Jill Levine, in the tradition of C. G. Montefiore and others, provides a lively elaboration of the difficulties encountered in attempting to apply directly to contemporary lives knowledge of the historical Jesus supplied by historical study. And finally James H. Charlesworth takes us through the issues of sources and methods involved in questing after Jesus and offers a provocative outline of just what might be the result of such a study.

It is altogether a choice feast for hungry readers.

WALTER P. WEAVER

Florida Southern College
Lakeland

Chapter 1

Why Is Historical Jesus Research Necessary?

John Dominic Crossan

Prologue: The Aesop Fallacy

There are four questions to be asked concerning the historical Jesus: why, where, how, and what? First, *why* should anyone be interested in the historical Jesus? Is not the Gospel Jesus or the New Testament Jesus or the Jesus of two thousand years of Christian faith the proper subject of discussion, and is not emphasis on the Jesus of history but avoidance of that deeper confrontation? Second, *where* does one get materials for such research? Is it only in the four intracanonical gospels and other texts within the present New Testament, or does it include extracanonical gospels and texts, such as the *Gospel of Thomas,* the *Gospel of Peter,* and the *Didache,* all discovered within the last 100 to 125 years? Third, *how* does one use such texts to distinguish the multiple layers of the Jesus tradition? What method establishes the historical stratum that derives from Jesus, the

Another written version of this original lecture appears now in *The Birth of Christianity* (San Francisco: HarperSanFrancisco, 1998) 19–46.

7

traditional stratum that adopted, adapted, and created materials from him and about him, and the evangelistic stratum that brought all of that into vital conjunction with the time and place of different Christian communities? Fourth, *what* does anyone get, finally, from all that study? What is one's reconstruction of the historical Jesus?

This chapter concerns itself exclusively with that first question, and it offers three reasons for such historical Jesus research: a historical, an ethical, and a theological reason. The first two reasons could be of interest to anyone, inside or outside the Christian community. The third and final one is only of concern within the Christian community, and it asks specifically, Is historical Jesus *research* necessary for Christian *faith?* My answer will be: for one type of Christian faith, no; for another type of Christian faith, yes. Those twin types will be identified as I proceed. But before considering each of those reasons in turn, I introduce you to the Aesop fallacy or, more neutrally, the Aesop affair.

The Aesopians have descended in unbroken continuity across two and a half millennia, holding their founder's fables as sacred scripture. Some of them claim that, at one time, all animals everywhere conversed easily with themselves and with humans. That golden age is long since gone, and many today connect its loss with ecological brutality on our part. Others, however, assert that it was only a special and unique intervention by Zeus that allowed certain animals to converse at that one and only time in ancient Greece. There are also many anti-Aesopians, who either cite Aesop as a very foolish ex-slave for making such claims or as a very smart ex-slave for using a special literary form to poke subversive criticism at the strong and the powerful. In the last few months, the Aesopians have sued the anti-Aesopians for defamation of faith, and the latter, having lost their case, were forced to pay huge fines, indemnities, and penalties. The victorious Aesopian lead-lawyer, Jimmy Coughlin, argued that none of the anti-Aesopians had lived in ancient Greece and could not possibly know what happened where they were not present. Furthermore, their claims that no animals anywhere had ever so acted were simply prejudice and presupposition. They had not checked all animals at all times and had not, in fact, even checked all animals presently alive. Asked after the verdict what they would do next, the jury said that they were going to Disney World.

I ask you to keep this parable in mind as you consider the following reasons why historical Jesus research is necessary.

The Historical Reason

The first reason is historical, and in theory, it should be the simplest of all. It is the Mallory principle but applied to historical figures rather than high altitudes. People climb Everest because it is there, an aphorism that cost Mallory his life. People study Jesus because he is there. Jesus and his first companions are historical figures and can be studied historically by anyone with the appropriate competence. That says no more or less about them than could be said about Socrates and his opponents or about Julius Caesar and his assassins. But there are complications with this reason, some concerning history and others concerning Jesus.

With Regard to History

First, there is always, of course, a general difficulty when contemporary present looks at distant past. It is not that *we* are that different from *them*, as if all of *us* were a single unified *we* and all of *them* a single unified *they*. There is probably as much divergence among modern us as there ever was among ancient them. Two individuals from different locations in our present contemporary world may be far more distant from one another than two individuals from different times in ancient and modern worlds. That is not the problem. The problem is that *we* know what happened, we know how it all turned out, at least from then to now. *We* know the future of *their* past.

How, for example, do we reconstruct the crucifixion of Jesus as if we did not know Gospel descriptions, artistic visualizations, musical celebrations, and two thousand years of Christian worship? What makes it all even, of course, is that we do not know the future of our own present. Only that awareness can make us internalize both their ignorance of past to present and our own of present to future. But that is only the general problem and general gift of any ancient history. It points, however, towards the more specific question, What is history itself?

Second, then, imagine two alternative and opposite modes of historical reconstruction, one an impossible delusion, the other a possible illusion. The possible illusion is *narcissism*. We think we are seeing the past or the other when all we see is our own reflected present. We see only our own face. We imprint our own present on the past and call it history. Narcissism sees its own face and, ignoring the water that shows it up, falls in love with itself. The impossible delusion is *positivism*. It imagines that we can know the past without any interference from our own personal and social situation as knower. We can see, as it were, without our own eyes being involved. We can discern the past once and for all forever and see it pure and uncontaminated by that discernment. Positivism is the delusion that we can see the water without our own face being mirrored in it. It thinks we can see the surface without simultaneously seeing our own eyes.

There is, however, a third mode of historical reconstruction, and I'll call it *interactivism*. The past and present must interact with one another, each changing and challenging the other, and the ideal is an absolutely fair and equal reaction between the two. Recall the waters of Narcissus. We cannot see the surface without simultaneously seeing, disturbing, and distorting our own face. We cannot see our own face without simultaneously seeing, disturbing, and distorting the surface. That is the dialectic of interactivism, and as distinct from either narcissism or positivism, it is both possible and necessary. It is, of course, a *method* that seeks to keep interaction between past and present as fairly equal as humanly possible.

This, therefore, is my working definition of history: *History is the past reconstructed interactively by the present through argued evidence in public discourse.* There are times we can only get alternative perspectives on the same event. And there are always alternative perspectives even when we do not hear them. But history as argued public reconstruction is possible because it is necessary. We reconstruct our past to project our future. And it is, unfortunately, *not* possible *not* to do it. But there is a tendency, in both contemporary culture and biblical exegesis, to avoid history by emphasizing story, to focus on the narrative and refrain from asking whether it is factual or fictional narrative.

In his book on the neurophysiology and sociopsychology of memory, Daniel L. Schacter tells the following rather horrible anecdote from the recent memory wars in the United States:

> A young woman named Ann described how she recovered in therapy memories of terrible satanic ritual abuse at the hands of her parents, and also discovered that she harbored multiple personalities. Family videotapes and photos showed Ann, prior to therapy, as a vibrant young woman and a budding young singer.... "I don't care if it's true," asserted Ann's therapist, Douglas Sawin. "What's important to me is that I hear the child's truth, the patient's truth. That's what's important. What actually happened is irrelevant to me." Asked about the possibility that a client's report is a delusion, Sawin did not flinch: "We all live in a delusion, just more or less delusionary."[1]

It is bad enough if such abuse happened to Ann; it is worse if it happened and no redress was possible. But it is surely worst of all, for herself, for her family, for her society, if her therapist finds the distinction between fact and fiction, fantasy and history, of no importance whatsoever. In telling that incident, Schacter footnoted that "objective or 'historical truth' ... becomes important when, as in Ann's case, a multimillion dollar law suit is filed against the alleged perpetrators."[2] But surely, even for therapy or especially for therapy, and apart from potential or actual lawsuits, there is a supreme difference between actual and delusional stories. And it is necessary to decide which is which. History matters. And history is possible because its absence is intolerable.

History is not the same as story. *Even if all history is story, not all story is history.* In the courtroom, with a famous athlete accused of double murder, the defense and the prosecution tell very different stories. In one he is a murderer who must be condemned. In the other he is an innocent who has been framed. The two lead lawyers are both highly competent and very entertaining storytellers, but only one of the two stories is history. The other is mistake, fiction, invention, lie. At the end, when the man walks out of the courtroom, he is either a freed murderer or a framed innocent. He cannot be both. Maybe we will never know for sure *which* version is history-story and which just story-story, but we know that only one version is correct. And our decency, morality, and humanity demand that we never say it is all relative, perspective, hype, and spin or that, since we cannot know for sure, it does not matter at all.

With Regard to Jesus

There is also a special problem when religious belief or disbelief, commitment or distaste, love or hate, is involved in historical reconstruction. Writing in 1906 when the search for the historical Jesus was already in middle course, Albert Schweitzer divided researchers into *haters* and *lovers*, "for hate as well as love can write a Life of Jesus." He first described the Jesus-haters:

> The greatest of them [the lives of Jesus] are written with hate.
> ...It was not so much hate of the Person of Jesus as of the supernatural nimbus with which it was so easy to surround Him, and with which He had in fact been surrounded. They were eager to picture Him as truly and purely human, to strip from Him the robes of splendour with which He had been apparelled, and clothe Him once more with the coarse garments in which He had walked in Galilee. And their hate sharpened their historical insight. They advanced the study of the subject more than all the others put together.

Schweitzer is speaking especially of Hermann Samuel Reimarus, who lived from 1694 to 1768 but was published anonymously only after his death. He is also speaking of David Friedrich Strauss, who lived from 1808 to 1874 but was published at the start of his university career, an achievement that immediately ended it. Schweitzer next described the Jesus-lovers:

But the others, those who tried to bring Jesus to life at the call of love, found it a cruel task to be honest. The critical study of the life of Jesus has been for theology a school of honesty.... It was fortunate for these men that their sympathies sometimes obscured their critical vision, so that, without becoming insincere, they were able to take white clouds for distant mountains.[3]

Are hate and love, polemics and apologetics, the inevitable alternatives for historical Jesus research, and if so, does not each option prejudice the evidence in equal but opposite directions? Jesus was received by both belief and disbelief, by both acceptance and indifference, by both worship and crucifixion. Is it not possible to bracket either response today and reconstruct what it would have been like to bracket it two thousand years ago? What did he say and do to beget such divergent responses?

I admit, finally, to suspecting those who insist that Jesus cannot be reconstructed historically. I am equally suspicious whether that assertion is made openly and initially or is the implicit conclusion to listing all the difficulties involved. Why is he, alone of all the past, so covered by a cloud of unknowing and a cloak of protective invisibility? That assertion of historical agnosticism seems but a negative way of asserting unique status and transcendental dignity. If Jesus is but a figure like Zeus, historical reconstruction is quite obviously absurd. If Jesus is but a figure like Hamlet, historical reconstruction is equally absurd. The former lives only in myth; the latter, only in literature. Jesus may also live in both those realms, but he also lived in history. Or that, at least, is the first historical question to be asked about him.

The Ethical Reason

The second reason is ethical, and it has to do with the morality of interpretation. It challenges alike both the pro-Christian apologist and the anti-Christian polemicist. It asks this question: Are we explaining now exactly what those ancient texts intended then? Before we agree or disagree with them, are we careful enough in deciding what they intended to assert? How, in other words, does the Aesop fallacy look as applied to the Christian Gospels?

There are both historical accounts and theological accounts about Jesus in the Gospels. That Jesus is the son of Mary is a historical statement of fact. That Jesus is the Son of God is a theological statement of faith. But there are also parabolic accounts, that is, theological claims formulated as if they were historical accounts. They are, in the terms used earlier, story but not history. Examples of such parabolic accounts are the walking on the waters and the miraculous catch of fish. Are those accounts historical or parabolic stories? Are they historical? That is to say, could anyone present have observed those events? Or are they parabolic? That is to say, are they theological claims in narratival format asserting that, without Jesus, the disciples row all night and get nowhere, fish all night and catch nothing, but as soon as Jesus joins them, they arrive safely at their destination and catch immediately more fish than they can handle?

It is ethically necessary for us Christians to state clearly and publicly when, on the one level, the Evangelists are giving historical, theological, or parabolic accounts and when, on the other level, we are reading them as historical, theological, or parabolic accounts. I think we Christians have hedged unethically about those distinctions, sometimes in theory but even more often in practice, and historical Jesus research challenges us to confront this problem in public discourse. Christianity has always claimed a historical basis, so this reason presses. In our Gospels, when are *they* making and *we* reading historical statements and when are *they* making and *we* reading parabolic ones? Those two italicized words underline the twin aspects of my ethical reason for historical Jesus research.

Consider now a more profoundly significant account than the two about water-walking and fish-catching just cited. My major question is this, Are we sure that ancient authors meant by such accounts exactly what we now understand them to say? I submit as an example the divine-human conception that started Jesus' earthly life, which is told by the evangelist Luke writing in the 80s of the first century. It is a miracle of divine and human conjunction, a child conceived from a divine father and a human mother. The conception occurs, as found in Luke 1:26–35, without the participation of any human father:

> In the sixth month the angel Gabriel was sent by God to a town in Galilee called Nazareth, to a virgin engaged to a man whose name was Joseph, of the house of David. The virgin's name was Mary. And he came to her and said, "Greetings, favored one! The Lord is with you." But she was much perplexed by his words and pondered what sort of greeting this might be. The angel said to her, "Do not be afraid, Mary, for you have found favor with God. And now, you will conceive in your womb and bear a son, and you will name him Jesus. He will be great, and will be called the Son of the Most High, and the Lord God will give to him the throne of his ancestor David. He will reign over the house of Jacob forever, and of his kingdom there will be no end." Mary said to the angel, "How can this be, since I am a virgin?" The angel said to her, "The Holy Spirit will come upon you, and the power of the Most High will overshadow you; therefore the child to be born will be holy; he will be called Son of God."

The text from Luke 1 makes claims that are historical, that are empirically verifiable, at least in part and in principle. It does not just speak of God but of a Mary who belongs to this earth and to its history. How does the historian respond? One reaction is to insist that any negation is just as theological as affirmation and that neither is historically acceptable. Historical reconstruction must stand mute before such transcendental claims. They are beyond historical verification or falsification, and the proper reaction is to bracket them historically without either affirming or denying them. The other reaction is that there has never been adequate empirical proof for such claims throughout past or present history and that the story, or others like it, should not be taken literally. It asserts certain physical consistencies for which exceptions would have to be publicly proved rather than privately asserted. Hold any decision between those two positions and read this second story.

The conception of Octavian, Augustus-to-be, is recorded by the Roman historian Suetonius in his *Lives of the Caesars*, which he wrote during the first quarter of the second century.[4] This divine conception took place over half a century before that of

Jesus. As he prepares to narrate the emperor's death, Suetonius pauses to record the omens that indicated Octavian's great destiny in birth, life, as well as death. This is how his mother Atia conceived him, as found in *The Deified Augustus* 94.4:

> When Atia had come in the middle of the night to the solemn service of Apollo, she had her litter set down in the temple and fell asleep, while the rest of the matrons also slept. On a sudden a serpent glided up to her and shortly went away. When she awoke, she purified herself, as if after the embraces of her husband, and at once there appeared on her body a mark in colors like a serpent, and she could never get rid of it; so that presently she ceased ever to go to the public baths. In the tenth month after that Augustus was born and was therefore regarded as the son of Apollo.

Augustus came from a miraculous conception by the divine and human conjunction of Apollo and Atia. How does the historian respond to this story? Are there any who take it literally or even bracket its transcendental claims as beyond historical judgment or empirical test? Classical historians, no matter how religious, do not usually do so. That divergence raises an ethical problem for me. Either all such divine conceptions, from Alexander to Augustus and from the Christ to the Buddha, should be accepted literally and miraculously, or all of them should be accepted metaphorically and theologically. It is not morally acceptable to say directly and openly that our story is truth but yours is myth, that ours is history but yours is lie. It is even less morally acceptable to say that indirectly and covertly by manufacturing defensive or protective strategies that apply only to one's own story.

This, then, is my problem, and I repeat that it is an ethical one. Anti-Christian or direct rationalism says that certain things cannot or, more wisely, do not happen. They are so far beyond the publicly verifiable or objectively provable consistencies of our world that, whatever their value as myth or parable, fable or story, they are not to be taken as fact, event, or history. It is easy, of course, to mock that attack, but we all live by it every day, especially where others are involved. (Where are you on aliens or Elvis?) Pro-Christian or indirect rationalism admits that those same types of events usually do not occur but insists that in one absolutely unique instance they did. A divine conception or a bodily resurrection, for example, has happened literally only once in the whole history of the world. To Jesus. Is that what those ancient texts intended to say?

The first century not only lacked a clear separation of Church and state; it also lacked a clear separation of heaven and earth. The pro-Christian defender Justin Martyr, writing his *First Apology* in the middle of the second century, and the anti-Christian attacker Celsus, writing his *On the True Doctrine* about twenty-five years later, had to agree therefore on this major point: virginal conception and divine impregnation at the start of a life or risen apparition and heavenly ascension at the end of a life are accepted possibilities of their cultural environment. Neither writer claimed that such events could not happen. Neither writer claimed that such events were unique. This is Justin's somewhat stunning assertion in his *First Apology* 21–22:

> And when we say also that the Word, who is the first-birth of God, was produced without sexual union, and that He, Jesus Christ, our Teacher, was crucified and died, and rose again, and ascended into heaven, we propound nothing different from what you believe regarding those whom you esteem sons of Jupiter. For you know how many sons your esteemed writers ascribed to Jupiter: Mercury...Aesculapius...Bacchus...Hercules...the sons of Leda, and Dioscuri...Perseus...Bellerophon...Ariadne. ...And what of the emperors who die among yourselves, whom you deem worthy of deification, and in whose behalf you produce someone who swears he has seen the burning Caesar rise to heaven from the funeral pyre?...But if any one objects that He was crucified, in this also He is on a par with those reputed sons of Jupiter of yours, who suffered....For their sufferings at death are recorded to have been not all alike, but diverse; so that not even by the peculiarity of His sufferings does He seem to be inferior to them....And in that we say that He made whole the lame, the paralytic, and those born blind, we seem to say what is very similar to the deeds said to have been done by Aesculapius.[5]

Of course, Christians argued that, with regard to the climactic case of Jesus, those pagan parallels were either created by God to prepare Christian faith or devised by Satan to confuse Christian faith. Still the argument could not be, in pro-Christian apologetics, that the case of Jesus was unique nor, in anti-Christian polemics, that such an event could not happen. Here, for example, is the best that Celsus did to refute Christian claims about Jesus' divine conception and bodily resurrection in his *On the True Doctrine,* as reconstructed from Origen's response:

> Are we to think that the high God would have fallen in love with a woman of no breeding? ... After all, the old myths of the Greeks that attribute a divine birth to Perseus, Amphion, Aeacus and Minos are equally good evidence of their wondrous works on behalf of mankind — and are certainly no less lacking in plausibility than the stories of your followers. What have you done [Jesus] by word or deed that is quite so wonderful as those heroes of old? ... Has there ever been such an incompetent planner: When he was in the body, he was disbelieved but preached to everyone; after his resurrection, apparently wanting to establish a strong faith, he chooses to show himself to one woman and a few comrades only. When he was punished, everyone saw; yet risen from the tomb, almost no one.[6]

Those are good cracks but weak criticisms. In a world where gods and goddesses, spirits and immortals, regularly interacted physically, sexually, spiritually, and intellectually with human beings, the divine conception of a human child and the risen apparition of a dead person are neither totally abnormal nor completely unique events.

We know from the above examples, and dozens of others like them, that the earliest Christians lived in a world not yet bedeviled by either direct or indirect rationalism, in a world where divine conceptions were quite acceptable, where, in fact, divine and human, eternal and temporal, heaven, earth, and hades, were marvelously porous and open to one another. *They* could never have argued that Jesus was uniquely unique because that conception had happened to him alone in all the world. They could not, and they did not. That is the second and more fundamental aspect of the ethical problem. When *we* read *them* as saying that the historical Jesus is uniquely unique and that such events happened only to him, *we* are misreading *them.* But, let me be very clear, they were making claims for their Jesus, and those claims were comparative over against all other such claims. That was precisely their point. Where, they asked, do *you* find the divine especially, particularly, or even uniquely present? Is it, for example, in Augustus, a Roman emperor backed by fabulous colonial wealth and massive military power, or in Jesus, a Jewish peasant child poor enough to be born in somebody else's stable? Where do *you* find your God? Choose.

We cannot live without group ideology (or, if you prefer, theology), but we must be able to keep it in dialectic with public evidence if, that is, we make claims to such data. My own position as a historian trying to be ethical and a Christian trying to be faithful is this: I do not accept *either* the divine conception of Jesus *or* Augustus as factual history, but I *believe* that God is incarnate in the Jewish peasant poverty of Jesus and not in the Roman imperial power of Augustus. I believe that, however, because of how Jesus lived and died (that is, in nonviolent resistance to systemic evil), not because of how he was conceived or born. Life, for me, is incarnation. Conception, for me, is parable, as it was, I think, for those ancient writers as well. The case is not that they told silly stories and that we got smart enough after the Enlightenment to understand them. The case is that they told profound parables and that we got dumb enough after the Enlightenment to misunderstand them.

The Theological Reason

The third reason is theological, and I offer it as a Christian to my fellow Christians and within the specific model of the New Testament Gospels themselves. This is for me the most important reason why historical Jesus research is necessary. I propose it as a challenge within Christian faith, within the Christian canon, and within Christian theology. It is based quite deliberately and conservatively on the nature of the canonical gospels. In preparation for what follows, I make two preliminary points.

First, why do you think we have four different gospels in our present New Testament canon? Was it not obvious from the very beginning that such a situation invited close-reading comparisons that could then emphasize disagreements and contradictions and generate mockery and dismissal? Would it not have been better, as proposed already in the second century, either to eliminate three and retain only one gospel, with Marcion, or to laminate all four into a single supergospel, with Tatian? Why was it important to keep multiple gospels in the emerging canon?

Second, I ask, more narrowly, about the necessity of historical Jesus research for Christian faith and not, more widely, about the necessity of the historical Jesus for Christian faith. One could reply affirmatively to that latter question and intend by it the real Jesus known only to God or the Gospel Jesus known only to faith. That is not my focus. I ask, Is *reconstructing* the historical Jesus necessary for Christian faith?

A Deep Fissure in Western Sensibility

Some background is necessary for what follows. It concerns a deep fissure in Western sensibility, reaching back at least to the time of Plato and continuing apace in contemporary North American life. In the ancient world, it cuts across the human person in paganism, Judaism, and Christianity. In the modern world, it cuts across the human person wherever flesh is separated from spirit, flesh is then sensationalized, spirit is then sentimentalized, and both are thereby dehumanized. There are different ways of articulating that fissure, and I indicate two before suggesting a third and more accurate one for my present discussion.

Kurt Rudolph described this fissure in terms of *gnosis* against *Church*, but that focuses primarily on Christianity and describes it as an outside attack against the Church rather than as an inside dispute within the Church:

> "Gnosis" or "Gnosticism" is [a]...form of religion in late antiquity....A clear-cut definition of this "religion of knowledge" or of "insight," as the Greek word *gnosis* may be translated, is not easy, but should at least be briefly suggested at the very

outset. We shall not go far wrong to see in it a dualistic religion, consisting of several schools and movements, which took up a definitely negative attitude towards the world and the society of the time, and proclaimed a deliverance ("redemption") of man precisely from the constraints of earthly existence through "insight" into his essential relationship, whether as "soul" or "spirit," — a relationship temporarily obscured — with a supramundane realm of freedom and of rest. [It] spread through time and space, from the beginning of our era onwards, from the western part of the Near East (Syria, Palestine, Egypt, Asia Minor)....One can almost say that Gnosis followed the Church like a shadow; the Church could never overcome it, its influence had gone too deep. By reason of their common history they remain two — hostile — sisters.[7]

Daniel Boyarin described the fissure in terms of both Judaism and Christianity but with a special focus on Paul in Galatians 3:28 ("There is no longer Jew or Greek, there is no longer slave or free, there is no longer male and female; for all of you are one in Christ Jesus"). Boyarin traces the fissure to a dualism of flesh and spirit derived from a pervasive Platonism in Paul's contemporary culture rather than from gnosticism:

Paul was motivated by a Hellenistic desire for the One, which among other things produced an ideal of a universal human essence, beyond difference and hierarchy. This universal humanity, however, was predicated (and still is) on the dualism of the flesh and the spirit, such that while the body is particular, marked through practice as Jew or Greek, and through anatomy as male or female, the spirit is universal. Paul did not, however, reject the body — as did, for instance, the gnostics — but rather promoted a system whereby the body had its place, albeit subordinated to the spirit....Various branches of Judaism (along with most of the surrounding culture) became increasingly platonized in late antiquity. By platonization I mean here the adoption of a dualist philosophy in which the phenomenal world was understood to be the representation in matter of a spiritual or ideal entity which corresponded to it. This has the further consequence that a hierarchical opposition is set up in which the invisible, inner reality is taken as more valuable or higher than the visible outer form of reality. In the anthropology of such a culture, the human person is constituted by an outer physical shell which is non-essential and by an inner spiritual soul, which represents his [sic] true and higher essence.[8]

The hierarchical dualism of spirit over flesh formed a spectrum from bodily neglect through bodily denigration to bodily rejection. The flesh could be to the spirit as its distracting mansion, its nomadic tent, its decrepit abode, or its filthy prison cell. Those were all points, however, along the same dualistic scale. Boyarin insists that Paul was not as radically dualistic as were some gnostics but had "as thoroughgoing a dualism as that of Philo," the contemporary Jewish philosopher from Alexandria; that is, "the body, while necessarily and positively valued by Paul is, as in Philo, not the human being but only his or her house or garment." Paul's dualism, in other words, "does not imply a rejection of the body"; it "does not abhor the body"; it "makes room for the body, however much the spirit is more highly valued."[9] Paul stands, however, on a very slippery Hellenistic slope. Finally, Boyarin concludes with this fundamental challenge. Because that "common dualist ideology...has characterized western thought practically since its inception," there "is...nothing striking in claiming that Paul was such a dualist; if anything, the bold step that I am making is to claim that the Rabbis (as opposed to both earlier Hellenistic Jews and later ones) *resisted* this form of dualism." But, "of course," he says, "the Rabbis also believed in a soul that animates the body. The point is, rather, that they identified the human being not as a soul dwelling in a body but as a body animated by a soul, and that makes all the difference in the world."[10] It does indeed.

That dichotomy between a monism of necessarily enfleshed spirit and a dualism of accidentally enfleshed spirit needs some precise descriptive terminology. If we are talking only about Christianity, it underlies Rudolph's distinction of gnosis against Church. It also underlies the more accurate distinction of gnostic Christianity against Catholic Christianity that emphasizes that both are options *within* the Church and *within* Christianity, until, at least, one has the power to declare the other heretical and itself orthodox. But that latter formulation has become so contaminated by apologetics and polemics, by accusations of heresy and claims of orthodoxy, that it is no longer helpful except for name-calling. That underlying dichotomy is, in any case, far older and wider than Christianity. It was there, as Boyarin noted, between traditional and Hellenistic Judaism before Christianity ever existed. And it is here today, as I suggested earlier, wherever flesh is separated from spirit, flesh is then sensationalized, spirit is then sentimentalized, and both are thereby dehumanized. I call that monism of enfleshed spirit *sarcophilia* and that dualism of flesh against spirit *sarcophobia*, from the Greek roots for flesh (*sarx*), love (*philia*), and fear (*phobos*). The terms are created on the analogy of *sarcophagus*, the marble coffin of antiquity, from flesh (*sarx*) and eat (*phagein*). We are dealing, therefore, with a profound fault line in Western consciousness, with the great divide between a sarcophilic and a sarcophobic sensibility. A coin has two sides, which can be distinguished but not separated (although, as I recall, Jorge Luis Borges once wrote of a one-sided coin!). Are flesh and spirit like the two sides of an inseparable coin or the two parts of a separable package?

In case that distinction is too abstract, here is a rather stunning example of sarcophobic sensibility, of the spirit's transcendence over the body, and of the flesh's irrelevance to the soul. It is a speech placed by Josephus on the lips of Eleazar, leader of the besieged rebels atop Masada at the end of the First Roman War in 74 C.E. The Romans under Flavius Silva had built up a huge ramp against the isolated mesalike rock fortress, and the end was now in sight. The defenders decided to kill their families and then themselves. Eleazar encourages them to prefer death to slavery:

> For it is death which gives liberty to the soul and permits it to depart to its own pure abode, there to be free from all calamity; but so long as it is imprisoned in a mortal body and tainted with all its miseries, it is, in sober truth, dead, for association with what is mortal ill befits that which is divine. True, the soul possesses great capacity, even while incarcerated in the body; for it makes the latter its organ of perception, invisibly swaying it and directing it onward in its actions beyond the range of mortal nature. But it is not until, freed from the weight that drags it down to earth and clings about it, the soul is restored to its proper sphere, that it enjoys a blessed energy and a power untrammeled on every side, remaining, like God Himself, invisible to human eyes.[11]

That speech, of course, is not Eleazar speaking to his fellow rebels but Josephus speaking to his fellow Romans. But it is hard to find a more precise formulation of the superiority of soul over body and of spirit over flesh.

In summary, then, the anti-body viewpoint, body-against-spirit disjunction, or sarcophobic sensibility involved a spectrum from the flesh as irrelevant or unimportant for the spirit, through the flesh as an impediment or distraction for the spirit, to the flesh as inimical or evil for the spirit. At one end of that spectrum was a philosophical anthropology negating flesh as the clinging distraction or degrading downfall of spirit. At the other end of the spectrum was a mythical cosmology negating flesh as the stultifying narcosis or evil opponent of spirit. The pro-body viewpoint, body-and-spirit conjunction, or sarcophilic sensibility opposed that spectrum at whatever point was appropriate for debate.

But, next, there was another disjunction built upon that preceding one. It compounds it, interacts with it, but could exist without it, all by itself. That disjunction of sarcophilic and sarcophobic understanding, as philosophical options in general sensibility, intertwined with the disjunction of an incarnational or docetic understanding, as theological options in specific Christology. And that also requires some background.

Some moderns may live in a world where immortal and mortal, heavenly and earthly, divine and human, are rather transcendentally separated from one another. Not so, in general, for the ancients. Their world was filled with gods, goddesses, and spirits who assumed divergent shapes and figures, who assumed and changed bodies as we assume clothes and change styles. Gods and goddesses, for example, could appear in any material, animal, or human form appropriate for the occasion. But all such bodies were not *really* real. They were only *apparently* real. They were like the interchangeable puppets of a single puppeteer. Could and did gods or goddesses become incarnate? Of course. They did so regularly, differently, and realistically, so that mortals could not recognize the unreality of those apparitional, illusional bodies. But did they really become incarnate? Of course not! In Augustan mythological propaganda the divine Aphrodite could bear Aeneas to the human Anchises or the human Atia could bear Octavian to the divine Apollo. No doubt appropriate human bodies were supplied for such divine-human relationships, but were those divinities really incarnate? Of course not.

The irrelevance of human flesh, on the one hand, and the unreality of divine flesh, on the other, presented earliest Christianity with a serious and profound problem concerning Jesus. Those believers were poised on that giant fault line in the ancient world, a fault line that involved the whole material world and all humans in it but that was now focused on Jesus. We might think to ourselves: Of course Jesus was human; the question is, Was he divine? They had the opposite problem. If you believed Jesus was divine, the question became, How could he be human? How could his body be real rather than apparitional and illusional? Was it not just a seem-to-be body? There was no point in responding that people saw, heard, or even touched his body. For all those things could be, as it were, arranged by resident divinity. This, then, was the problem.

If Jesus was divine, was his body real and *incarnational* in the sense of fully and validly enfleshed, or was his body unreal and apparitional, only seemingly enfleshed, a *docetic* body (from Greek *dokein*, "to seem")? If, in other words, we are talking only about Christ, that fissure of sarcophilic against sarcophobic sensibility underlies the distinction between incarnational and docetic Christology. The former gives Jesus a full, normal, human body; the latter gives him only an apparent body. All that is background; now for the foreground, for the theological and canonical reason why historical Jesus research is necessary for Christian faith.

Before proceeding, a short time-out for confession is required. I admit immediately that my own philosophical position is irrevocably within sarcophilic rather than sarcophobic sensibility and that my own theological position is irrevocably within incarnational rather than docetic Christology. But I can make that admission without denying Christian status to sarcophobic and/or docetic Christians, without describing them unfairly or unjustly, and without thinking that persecution, then or now, is the best form of persuasion. Finally, I think that the dualism of spirit against flesh dehumanizes the person and that dualism dehumanizes the person further when spirit somehow becomes male and flesh somehow becomes female. How do you understand a human being?

A Fourfold Typology of Gospels

I ask you, first, to consider four different *types* of gospels, four different ways of telling the Jesus story within early Christianity. It is not just a case of four different gospels, like Matthew, Mark, Luke, and John within the present New Testament canon. It is a case of four different *types* with those four canonical gospels as but one single type. Note the following three preliminaries. I deliberately use the rather vague term "types," rather than the more precise term "genres," because there may be several different genres involved in a given type. Also, there is an emphasis not just on content but even more especially on form and, indeed, on the point where form becomes content, where the medium becomes the message. Finally, it is not significant for my present concern whether or not a given text explicitly calls itself a gospel. What is important is what type of text is used to tell the story of Jesus as Good News. I give each type a descriptive title.

Sayings Gospels

The first type, sayings gospels, includes collections primarily of the words of Jesus. These include aphorisms, parables, and short dialogues. Incidents, if they are present, emphasize the word rather than the deed. There are, for example, few miracle stories, no birth tales, no passion narratives, and no risen apparitions. The classic examples from the middle of the first century are the *Q Gospel* and the *Gospel of Thomas*. The former is a hypothetical written source discovered during the last century in the Gospels of Matthew and Luke. The latter is an actual written document discovered during this century in the sands of Egypt.

Biography Gospels

The second type, biography gospels, is represented by the four canonical gospels. I emphasize not only that there are four but that all belong to the same single type. In this set Jesus is located back in the late 20s of his first-century Jewish homeland, but he is also updated to speak or act directly and immediately to new situations and communities in the 70s, 80s, and 90s. There is an absolute lamination of Jesus-then and Jesus-now without any distinction of Jesus-said-then but Jesus-means-now. In Mark, for example, Jesus confesses and is condemned while Peter denies and is forgiven, but those specific events, although dated say to the year 30, speak directly and were created precisely for a persecuted community in the year 70. You should have behaved like Jesus, but even if you behaved like Peter, there is still mercy and forgiveness from Jesus himself. That is why those four gospels could be so different, even when they are copying from one another. Indeed, one might well wonder why they kept all four since anyone could see those quite obvious differences. The reason becomes clearer, however, when we consider the next type.

Discourse Gospels

The third type, discourse gospels, begins where the preceding type ends. While biography gospels detailed the life of Jesus and ended with his resurrection, discourse gospels began after his resurrection and went on from there. Jesus appears to the disciples, and the narrative continues in a mix of monologue and dialogue, of questions and answers between them and him. Two examples will suffice.

The first example is from one of the codices discovered at Nag Hammadi in 1945. It is translated by Francis Williams and dated by noting that "it is urged that the tractate must have been written before 150 C.E., while it was still possible to speak of 'remembering' orally delivered sayings of Jesus and writing them down; this language, it is argued, would not have been used after the fixing of the Gospel canon."[12] According to the *Apocryphon of James* 2.9–29:

> The twelve disciples [were] all sitting together and recalling what the Savior had said to each one of them, whether in secret or openly, and [putting it] in books — [But I] was writing that which was in [my book] — lo, the Savior appeared, [after] departing from [us while we] gazed after him. And five hundred and fifty days since he had risen from the dead, we said to him. . . . But Jesus said. . . . They all answered. . . . He said . . .

In discourse gospels, the risen Jesus speaks, and the disciples, especially Peter and James in this case, ask questions. But the striking feature is not just that dialogue or discourse phenomenon but that it all takes place after the Resurrection.

The second example, from another Nag Hammadi codex, is similarly set after the Resurrection, but now the questioners are Bartholomew, Mary, Matthew, Philip, and Thomas. It is translated by Douglas Parrott and dated to "soon after the advent of Christianity in Egypt — the latter half of the first century C.E."[13] This is *The Sophia of Jesus Christ* 90.14–92.6:

> After he rose from the dead, his twelve disciples and seven women continued to be his followers and went to Galilee onto the mountain . . . the Savior appeared, not in his previous form, but in the invisible spirit. And his likeness resembles a great angel of light. . . . And he said: "Peace be to you! My peace I give to you!" And they all marveled and were afraid. The Savior laughed and said. . . . Philip said. . . . The Savior said . . .

If biography gospels give us twenty chapters before the Resurrection, discourse gospels give us twenty chapters afterwards.

Biography-Discourse Gospels

The fourth and final type, biography-discourse gospels, emphasizes in that title its polemically hybrid aspect. Once again two examples will suffice, but the content of these two examples is very different. The first example is the *Epistle of the Apostles,* or

Epistula Apostolorum. Its content is within incarnational Christianity; its discourse part is far longer than its biography part, but it tries, as it were, to subsume discourse within biography. The second example is *John's Preaching of the Gospel.* Its content is within docetic Christianity; its biography part is slightly longer than its discourse part, but it tries, as it were, to subsume biography within discourse.

The first example is a Greek text, the *Epistle of the Apostles,* extant now primarily in Coptic and Ethiopic translations. It is translated by C. Detlef G. Muller and dated to "about the middle of the 2nd century."[14] It actually combines biography- and discourse-gospel models, although with far more space for the latter than the former. Of its fifty-one present units, only 3–12a summarize in swift outline the canonical gospel accounts of Jesus' words and deeds, life and death, burial and resurrection. This outline is actually a catalogue of miracles. It begins with the virginal conception and Bethlehem birth, mentions Jesus learning letters but knowing them already, and then goes on to recount the stories of the wedding at Cana, the woman with a hemorrhage, the exorcism of Legion into the swine, the walking on the waters, and the multiplication of loaves and fishes. It concludes with the Crucifixion under Pontius Pilate and Archelaus (Antipas?), the burial, the women at the tomb and Jesus' appearances to them, the disbelief of the disciples, and, finally, Jesus' appearance to them, despite the doubts of Peter, Thomas, and Andrew.

But all the rest, units 13–51, is a postresurrectional dialogue with repeated interchanges between the risen Jesus ("he said") and the apostles ("we said"). Here, in 12a, is the point where biography gospel converts smoothly into discourse gospel (*New Testament Apocrypha* 1.256):

> But we touched him that we might truly know whether he had risen in the flesh, and we fell on our faces confessing our sin, that we had been unbelieving. Then the Lord our redeemer said, "Rise up, and I will reveal to you what is above heaven and what is in heaven, and your rest that is in the kingdom of heaven. For my Father has given me the power to take up you and those who believe in me. . . . We answered. . . . Then he answered. . . . We said . . .

Jesus even foretells, in *Epistula Apostolorum* 31–33, that Paul would persecute the Church and be converted to become apostle to the pagans. The entire discourse section is between Jesus and the disciples as a choral "we" without any individuals singled out as questioners.

The second example of this hybrid type is a source usually called *John's Preaching of the Gospel*, which is now embedded in the *Acts of John* 87–105. It is translated by Knut Schäferdiek and dated to "the first half of the 3rd century,"[15] but Ronald Cameron has suggested "a date of composition early in the second century" for the specific section in *Acts of John* 87–105.[16] It is an extraordinarily beautiful text that merges those twin types of biography and discourse in a very special way.

In the first part, *Acts of John* 88b–96, the earthly life of Jesus is summarized but with emphasis on the unreality of his body. This is shown by four points, each of which is mentioned twice. First, Jesus' body is polymorphous and ever changing. The sons of Zebedee see Jesus on the shore, but at first James sees "a child," and John sees a "man...handsome, fair, and cheerful-looking." Later as they beach their boat, John sees Jesus as "rather bald-(headed) but with a thick flowing beard" while James now sees "a young man whose beard was just beginning." Next, John "never saw Jesus' eyes closing, but always open." One night, in fact, while John was faking sleep, he saw "another like him coming down" to Jesus. Furthermore, Jesus' body was both small and huge: "He sometimes appeared to me as a small man with no good looks, and then again as looking up to heaven." Thus, for example, on the Mount of Transfiguration, Jesus' "head stretched up to heaven," but when he turned about, he "appeared as [a] small man." Finally, Jesus' body "had another strange (property); when I reclined at table he would take me to his own breast, and I held him (fast); and sometimes his breast felt to me smooth and soft, but sometimes hard like rock." And again, a second time, "I will tell you another glory, brethren; sometimes when I meant to touch him I encountered a material, solid body; but at other times again when I felt him, his substance was immaterial and incorporeal, and as if it did not exist at all."

The second part, *Acts of John* 97–101, takes place at the Crucifixion itself. And in this gospel, consequent on that bodily unreality, it is not Jesus who suffers and dies except, as John insists, in symbol. This is the *Acts of John* 97:

> And so I saw him suffer, and did not wait by his suffering, but fled to the Mount of Olives and wept at what had come to pass. And when he was hung (upon the Cross) on Friday, at the sixth hour of the day there came a darkness over the whole earth. And my Lord stood in the middle of the cave and gave light to it and said, "John, for the people below in Jerusalem I am being crucified and pierced with lances and reeds, and given vinegar and gall to drink. But to you I am speaking, and listen to what I speak. I put into your mind to come up to this mountain so that you may hear what a disciple should learn from his teacher and a man from God."

That sounds like the postresurrectional Jesus beginning a standard discourse-type gospel, but in this instance pre-Easter and post-Easter have no meaning since there is only one Jesus who both is and is not ever embodied. In his explanation in the *Acts of John* 101, Jesus insists on this paradox:

> You hear that I suffered, yet I suffered not; and that I suffered not, yet I did suffer; and that I was pierced, yet I was not wounded; that I was hanged, yet I was not hanged; that blood flowed from me, yet it did not flow; and, in a word, that what they say of me, I did not endure, but what they do not say, those things I did suffer.

There are, Jesus explains, two crosses: the cross of wood, on which his unreality suffered, and the cross of light, on which his reality continues to suffer. The former is the transient passion of body. The latter is the permanent passion of God. God has been, as it were, dismembered, and his parts, like fragments of light, have been scattered within bodies here on earth. Until all those members return home, God is in passion, impaled, as it were, on a cross of light.

The third part, *Acts of John* 102–4, begins with the ascension of Jesus: "He was taken up, without any of the multitude seeing him." John then concludes with a commentary of his own. His basic interpretive principle is this: "I held this one thing fast in my (mind), that the Lord had performed everything as a symbol and a dispensation for the conversion and salvation of man." Hence those stunning paradoxes above: Jesus did not really suffer on the cross (of wood), but he always suffers on the cross (of light). And the former is the symbol of the latter. Similarly, says John, the present persecution of our bodies is important as a symbol for the persecution of our spirits. The former may place us on a cross of wood, but we are always, with God, on a cross of light. We are always part of the passion of God. Hence this profoundly beautiful and terribly poignant conclusion in the *Acts of John* 103:

> (Let us worship) him who was made man (apart from) this body.
> And let us watch, since he is at hand even now in prisons for
> our sakes, and in tombs, in bonds and dungeons, in reproaches
> and insults, by sea and on dry land, in torments, sentences, con-
> spiracies, plots and punishments; in a word, he is with all of us,
> and with the sufferers he suffers himself, (my) brethren.... being
> the God of those who are imprisoned, bringing us help through
> his own compassion.

That preceding gospel version might strike a contemporary reader as exceedingly strange, but that very strangeness reveals most clearly what is at stake in the fourfold typology.

A War of Gospel Types

The fourfold typology is not a placid inventory of gospel possibilities, but actually a war of gospel types. The center of the war is the clash between biography gospels and discourse gospels, but understanding what is at stake in that battle presumes all that was just seen about the fissure in Western history between a sarcophilic and sarcophobic sensibility and/or the fissure in Christian theology between an incarnational and docetic Jesus.

Those disjunctions explain how biography gospels, the programmatic gospels of sarcophilic and/or incarnational Christianity, and discourse gospels, the programmatic gospels of sarcophobic and/or docetic Christianity, opposed one another. They also explain how sayings gospels, which were earlier and could have moved in either direction, were doomed by that very ambiguity. They would end up incorporated into either of those opposing types: the *Q Gospel* was taken into Matthew and Luke, but the *Gospel of Thomas* was taken into the *Book of Thomas the Contender* and the *Acts of Thomas*.[17] Those disjunctions explain, finally, those hybrid biography-discourse gospels. On the one hand, the *Epistula Apostolorum* pulls discourse within biography. On the other hand, the *Acts of John* 87–105 pulls biography within discourse and has the earthly or biographical Jesus as unreal and docetic, albeit as symbolically significant, as one could imagine.

When, therefore, the canon contains four examples of the biography-gospel type, it makes normative not only those four but that very type. Biography gospels insist on the utter embodied historicity of Jesus, while discourse gospels find that emphasis radically misplaced. By the way, in case you still find this all very strange, let me ask you a question. If you were guaranteed five minutes with Jesus but had to choose between five from history long ago or five from heaven right now, which would you choose?

My challenge, then, is a theological one from within canonical normativity. How exactly are those four gospels as a single type normative for Christians who invoke their authority and seek to live within that heritage? It is not just their *content* that is normative but especially their very *form*. They are not simply four discourses by the risen Jesus, each giving absolutely orthodox and officially approved doctrines. Such texts, no matter how unimpeachable their content, were not canonically acceptable, and that decision was a fateful one for Christianity's future and my present concern with the historical Jesus. Each of those canonical gospels goes back to the historical Jesus of the late 20s in his Jewish homeland, but each of them has that Jesus speak directly to its own immediate situations and communities. In every case there is a dialectic of then-and-now, of then-as-now, that is, of the historical Jesus then as the risen Jesus now. It is not the historical Jesus alone then and not the risen Jesus alone now, but the two as one within a contemporary faith. It is *always* that same process but *always* with slightly or massively divergent products. Think, for example, of how differently the agony in the garden appears in Mark 14, which has no garden, and in John 18, which has no agony. But still that dialectic of then and now continues to hold. My proposal is that *the canonical gospel type is normative primarily as that dialectical process.* Those gospels always created an interaction of historical Jesus and risen Jesus, and that interaction must be repeated again and again throughout Christian history.

Epilogue: Word Made Flesh, Word Made Text

The Easter issues of *Newsweek* and *Time,* as well as *U.S. News & World Report,* April 8, 1996, all had cover stories on the historical Jesus. *Newsweek* had the caption "Rethinking the Resurrection: A New Debate about the Risen Christ." It was written across a picture of Jesus rising heavenwards, arms uplifted, hands facing outwards. What struck me immediately as strange was the complete absence of any wounds on those clearly visible hands and feet. I failed to realize that they had mistakenly taken Jesus from a Transfiguration instead of a Resurrection painting. There were, of course, no wounds on that Vatican work by Raphael because it depicted an event before the death of Jesus. *U.S. News & World Report,* on the other hand (no pun intended), had a correct picture. Its cover had the caption "In Search of Jesus: Who was he? New appraisals of his life and meaning?" written across Jesus from a Bellini painting of the Resurrection with the wound in Jesus' right hand clearly visible.

There is, I repeat, ever and always only one Jesus. For Christians, that is the historical Jesus *as* the risen Jesus. And the test is this: does the risen Jesus still carry the wounds of crucifixion? In Christian gospel, art, and mysticism, the answer is clearly yes. But those wounds are the marks of history. To understand them, you would have to know about his death. But to understand the death, you would have to know about his life, for otherwise he might have been a criminal meeting appropriate sentence or his executioners might have been savages operating from sheer random brutality. With those canonical gospels as inaugural models and primordial examples, each Christian generation must write its gospels anew — must first reconstruct its historical Jesus with fullest integrity and then say and live what that reconstruction means for present life in this world. History and faith are always a dialectic for incarnational Christianity. Put otherwise, its insistence on the Resurrection of Jesus' body is my insistence on the permanence of Jesus' history. But then, now, and always it is a history seen by faith.

Within Christianity, the Bible, the New Testament, and especially the Gospels are the Word of God made text, just as Jesus is the Word of God made flesh. It would have been quite possible for Christian tradition to have declared some one, single, given manuscript of the Bible to be official and canonical. Imagine that had happened, for example, to the Codex Vaticanus, a fourth-century vellum copy of 759 leaves, three columns per page, forty-two lines to the column. Imagine that had been declared to be the immutable and inspired Word of God, with its three-column page manifesting forever the mystery of the Trinity. There might have been discussion on what to do about the indignant scribe who added in the left-hand margin of Hebrews 1:3 this succinct comment on an earlier colleague's work: "Fool and knave, can't you leave the old reading alone, and not alter it."[18] It would make no difference what tattered fragments or total texts survived from earlier times in the Egyptian sands. It would make no difference what academic scholars or textual critics thought was historically a more accurate original text. The Codex Vaticanus would be it, once and for all forever. The Word of God made text would be safe from the vagaries of history, the excavations of archaeologists, and the surprise discoveries of peasants or shepherds.

Instead of that option, I have on my desk *The Greek New Testament* from the United Bible Societies. It gives the closest a committee can come to the original text with the alternative readings in footnote apparatus. It grades any disputed reading from A to D

> so as to mark one of four levels of certainty, as representing in large measure the difficulties encountered by the Committee

in making textual decisions. The letter A indicates that the text is certain. The letter B indicates that the text is almost certain. The letter C, however, indicates that the Committee had difficulty in deciding which variant to place in the text. The letter D, which occurs only rarely, indicates that the Committee had great difficulty in arriving at a decision.[19]

But fact and faith, history and theology, intertwine together in that process and cannot ever be totally separated.

As with the Word of God made text, so also with the Word of God made flesh. Historical reconstruction interweaves with Christian faith, and neither can substitute for the other. I insist, however, that it did not have to be that way. It is sarcophilic and/or incarnational as distinct from sarcophobic and/or docetic Christianity that gave out gages to materiality and hostages to history. It is now too late for it to repent, and I, for one, would not want it to do so. But I also wonder about this: Is the history of Christianity and especially of Christian theology the long, slow victory of sarcophobic and/or docetic sensibility over sarcophilic and/or incarnational sensibility?

Notes

1. Daniel L. Schacter, *Searching for Memory: The Brain, the Mind, and the Past* (New York: HarperCollins Basic Books, 1996) 262–63.

2. Ibid., 344 n. 28.

3. Albert Schweitzer, *The Quest of the Historical Jesus: A Critical Study of Its Progress from Reimarus to Wrede*, trans. William Montgomery, with intro. by James M. Robinson (New York: Macmillan, 1969) 4–5.

4. *Suetonius*, trans. John C. Rolfe, Loeb Classical Library (Cambridge: Harvard University Press, 1979) 2:264–67.

5. *The Ante-Nicene Fathers*, ed. Alexander Roberts, James Donaldson, and A. Cleveland Core (New York: Scribner, 1926) 1: 316–18.

6. *Celsus: On the True Doctrine*, trans. R. Joseph Hoffman (New York: Oxford University Press, 1987) 57–59, 68.

7. Kurt Rudolph, *Gnosis: The Nature and History of Gnosticism*, trans. R. McL. Wilson, P. W. Coxon, and K. H. Kuhn, ed. R. McL. Wilson (San Francisco: Harper and Row, 1983; from the German of 1977) 1–2, 368.

8. Daniel Boyarin, *A Radical Jew: Paul and the Politics of Identity*, Contraversions: Critical Studies in Jewish Literature, Culture, and

Society 1 (Berkeley: University of California Press, 1994) 7, 59 (*sic* original).

9. Ibid., 59, 64, 185.

10. Ibid., 85, 278 n. 8.

11. Josephus *Jewish War* 7.344–46. See *Josephus,* trans. Henry St. John Thackeray, Ralph Marcus, Allen Wikgren, and Louis H. Feldman, Loeb Classical Library (Cambridge: Harvard University Press, 1926–65) 3:601–3.

12. *The Nag Hammadi Library in English,* ed. James M. Robinson, 3d ed., completely rev. (Leiden: Brill, 1988) 30. For urgings and arguments, see Ronald D. Cameron, *Sayings Traditions in the Apocryphon of James,* Harvard Theological Studies 34 (Philadelphia: Fortress, 1984).

13. *Nag Hammadi Library,* 221–22.

14. *New Testament Apocrypha,* 2 vols., ed. Wilhelm Schneemelcher and R. McL. Wilson, rev. ed. (Louisville: Westminster/John Knox, 1991–92) 1:251, 256 (Coptic). See also Julian Hills, *Tradition and Composition in the Epistula Apostolorum,* Harvard Dissertations in Religion 24 (Minneapolis: Fortress, 1990).

15. *New Testament Apocrypha,* 2:167 (for date); 2:180–81, 184–86 (for texts cited).

16. *The Other Gospels: Non-Canonical Gospel Texts,* ed. Ronald D. Cameron (Philadelphia: Westminster, 1982) 88.

17. For those texts, see respectively *Nag Hammadi Library,* 199–207; *New Testament Apocrypha,* 2:322–411.

18. Bruce M. Metzger, *Manuscripts of the Greek Bible: An Introduction to Greek Palaeography* (New York: Oxford University Press, 1981) 74.

19. *The Greek New Testament,* ed. Barbara Aland and others, 4th rev. ed. (Stuttgart: United Bible Societies, 1993), 3*.

Chapter 2

How Do We Know
What We Know about Jesus?

E. P. Sanders

Introduction

The question, How do we know what we know
about Jesus? assumes that we do not gain adequate and reliable information by simply picking up the New Testament and
reading the Gospels. And this is in fact what New Testament
scholars have thought for at least 150 years: not all the passages
in the Gospels provide equally good information about the historical Jesus. While many readers already share this view, it is
nevertheless worth a few pages of explanation and elaboration,
partly to provide a "refresher course" and partly to explain why
we New Testament scholars do the things we do.

We face real problems when we try to describe Jesus. Christian believers (including priests, pastors, and ministers) may
or may not be keenly interested in the search for the historical Jesus. Since Christianity arose from certain historical events,
some degree of interest in this search is natural and proper. On
the other hand, Christian faith does not require any particular
solution to the various puzzles presented by the Gospels. I shall

say a few more words about this subject later in this chapter, but for now I wish only to register the point that I am writing about research — the problems that New Testament scholars meet and the solutions they devise. Research deals with probabilities, and it should not be able either to create or destroy faith; at its best, it can inform faith. Its actual task, however, is to illuminate the early period of the Christian movement for interested believers and unbelievers alike. Scholarship that *aims* at either supporting or damaging faith is, in my view, not true scholarship. Scholarship should be "disinterested," not the servant of a preferred set of conclusions.

Not only is this chapter not about Christian faith; it is also not a complete description of my view of the historical Jesus. As the title ("How Do We Know?") implies, I shall focus on historical problems and the methods designed to overcome them, and I shall not be able to give a very full account of what the conclusions are. I have several times offered descriptions of Jesus as I see him, and the present chapter is not a summary or replay of those descriptions, though a few key points will emerge.[1]

Moreover, in this chapter I shall principally discuss sayings. My own work on the historical Jesus has placed a little more emphasis on Jesus' symbolic actions and his miracles (collectively called his "deeds") than on sayings, but in the context of the subject proposed to me as my contribution it seemed right to focus on sayings. We begin with the difficulties involved in seeking good knowledge of the historical Jesus.

The Need to Analyze and Sift the Material

The difficulties will be best understood if we start with three basic facts about the early Christian movement. The first is that Jesus' disciples did not sit down immediately after the Resurrection and compose accounts of his life. They expected him shortly to return, and they went about trying to persuade people to believe in him and to await his return from heaven. We shall return to this expectation, and here I wish only to point out that it helps to account for the relatively late date of the

Gospels. The urgency of the missionary work of the first believers, which was partly based on the expectation that the Lord would soon return, meant that they had little reason to write biographies of Jesus, nor much time in which to do it. Jesus died in approximately the year 30. The missionary work of the first believers took place during the next three or four decades (from the 30s of the first century into the 60s). Scholars disagree somewhat about when the Gospels as we have them were written, but it was probably in the 70s and 80s, that is, forty or more years after Jesus' death.[2]

The second fact about early Christianity that bears on our topic is that the disciples and other missionaries quoted sayings by Jesus, or recalled some of the things that he had done, in the context of their own teaching and preaching. Paul's letters provide good examples. In 1 Corinthians 7, for example, he responds to a question about marriage. Apparently the Corinthians had asked him whether or not celibacy was better than marriage. (Paul himself seems to have been celibate, and that would have raised the question.) As part of his answer to this question, he comments on divorce, and he cites a version of Jesus' saying that prohibits divorce. From Paul's chapter, we have no idea in what context Jesus originally commented on divorce and remarriage. This illustrates the fact that although the early Christians made use of Jesus' teaching and frequently recalled his miracles and other deeds, the context was their own: they used traditions about Jesus for their present purposes and did not necessarily preserve the original context. I should add that the saying on divorce occurs in three different contexts in the Gospels, which confirms that we are uncertain of the original context of Jesus' sayings.[3]

The third basic fact about early Christianity is that the Christians believed that Jesus was alive in heaven and that they could communicate with him. They could, of course, address him in prayer and meditation. What is important for the present point is that he could answer them, and they could quote his answers. From Paul, again, we have absolutely firm evidence that this happened. In discussing the revelations that he had received from heaven and even in heaven, he wrote that the

Lord had kept him humble by giving him a "thorn in the flesh" (some torment that he does not specify). Three times, he wrote, he appealed to the Lord to take it away, and the Lord finally answered. He said, "My grace is sufficient for you, for my power is made perfect in weakness" (2 Cor 12:9). Here we have a brand-new saying, spoken not by the earthly Jesus but by the heavenly Lord. It does not take much imagination to see that a saying by the heavenly Lord might have worked its way into the Gospels as a saying by Jesus (though this one did not do so).

I shall say a few more words about the distinction between the earthly Jesus and the heavenly Lord. Today, almost everyone in the Western world and a lot of people in Asia would like to know what the historical Jesus was really like — as a man, what he said and did. Not everyone has a burning desire to know, but most people have at least some curiosity. For a lot of people, the historical Jesus stands as a partial alternative to the Christian Church, and so people sometimes tell me that they are not Christian, do not go to church, and do not pray, but find Jesus interesting and would like to know more about him. Some say that they would like to follow him, if only they could do so outside the confines of the Christian Church. This is actually in continuity with one of the motives behind the search for the historical Jesus in the late eighteenth and the nineteenth centuries: for many, the quest for the historical Jesus was an attempt to find a religious hero independent of what many people regarded as the dead hand of Christian dogma.

Thus I take it that millions of people would like to know what the historical Jesus did and said. Those of us who are Christian also care what the Lord's will is for us now, and most Christians seek to know his will by praying. Sometimes those who pray hear answers, as Paul did. But more or less all modern people — including those who talk to Jesus in prayer — would distinguish the historical, earthly Jesus from the heavenly Lord. The early Christians wanted to know the Lord's will, and to them the Lord was one: our neat division between earthly and heavenly was by no means so clear in the first century when it came to asking about Jesus. They of course could distinguish earth from heaven, but still they thought that the Lord was one.

From Paul's point of view, as we have just seen, "the Lord" told him that his grace was sufficient, just as "the Lord" told him that divorced people should not remarry. It was the same Lord who spoke. Now, however, when discussing Jesus, and meaning thereby the historical Jesus, we would attribute to him only the passage about divorce, not the statement about grace that Paul heard in prayer. Similarly the author of the Book of Revelation attributes to Jesus seven letters to seven churches in Asia (see 1:10–3:22). No modern scholar considers these letters when discussing Jesus, since they do not come from the historical Jesus. What this means is that we cannot assume that the early Christians meticulously made a distinction that is natural to us by separating what the historical Jesus said from what the Lord said when they prayed to him.

The early Christians also believed in prophecy. The Spirit inspired some people to prophesy, and the listeners may not have neatly distinguished "the Spirit" from "the Lord"; as Paul said on at least one occasion, "the Lord is the Spirit" (2 Cor 3:17). Thus Spirit-filled prophecy is another potential source of new sayings that were attributed to "the Lord" and then incorporated in the Gospels. If I wanted to put this provocatively, I would say that the early Christians sometimes made up sayings or events and attributed them to Jesus. This is tempting, but I think that this was not the way they saw it. They thought that the Lord or the Spirit still communicated. What scholars now think is that after these communications had been passed around by word of mouth for a while, some of them entered the Gospel material. We would now like to be able to distinguish them.

These basic facts about early Christianity give us various difficulties in finding out what Jesus was really like, what he said and what he did. I shall describe three things that we lack but that we would need in order to write a really full description of the historical Jesus.

No Eyewitness Accounts

We do not have an eyewitness account of Jesus' career that connects words and deeds to specific occasions. This follows from the fact that the followers of Jesus, after the Resurrection, did not immediately sit down and write a circumstantial life of Jesus. The Gospels do not give very much information about the specific occasions on which certain things happened. The first three Gospels (the "synoptic" Gospels) are composed of brief snippets of material that have been moved around and used in various contexts. The Gospels sometimes give virtually no context at all. When they give one, we cannot know whether or not it is the original context.

If, for example, we read Mark 2:1–3:6, we see a series of five conflict stories with the briefest of introductions. According to the first, Jesus returned to Capernaum, a lot of people gathered, he healed a paralytic, and some people raised questions in their hearts. Jesus answered the unspoken questions; the story ends. Second: Jesus saw a toll collector, then went home and dined with him; scribes of the Pharisees appeared at the dinner and asked the disciples why Jesus ate with sinners. He answered; the story ends. Third: John's disciples and the Pharisees were fasting; someone asked Jesus why his disciples did not fast. Jesus answered; the story ends. Fourth: one sabbath Jesus and his followers were walking through grainfields. His disciples plucked grain and ate; Pharisees emerged and challenged them for working on the sabbath. Jesus answered; the story ends. Finally (fifth), we read, "Again he entered the synagogue"; then he healed a man with a withered hand and defended himself for healing on the sabbath (though no objection was raised out loud). The Pharisees and Herodians plotted against him, and the story ends.

I would like to know all kinds of things about these stories. Why did scribes of Pharisees appear at the dinner with toll collectors? What was wrong with what Jesus was doing? What did the scribes of the Pharisees think about the event later? Or, with regard to the grainfield, why were Jesus and his disciples traveling on the sabbath? Why did they not have any food? Had their host of the previous evening not prepared food for them in advance? How far were they from the nearest town or village? Why were Pharisees camped out in the grainfields? Did all Pharisees spend the sabbath in grainfields? When did

they study and instruct their children? Were they satisfied with
Jesus' answer? Did they report his disciples to the local mag-
istrate? And about all the passages, I would ask: Why were his
opponents so easily silenced? Could they not argue back at least
a little? The Pharisees were learned, and scribes were learned.
Therefore scribes of Pharisees must have known a lot. So why
did they give up without an argument?

There are also questions with regard to Mark's simple listing of these stories one after another. The most obvious one
is this: What were Jesus and his disciples doing between con-
flicts? Presumably his life did not actually consist of one conflict
immediately followed by another. Several times Mark indicates
that these events were separated by some time: "again" appears
in 2:1, 13; 3:1. The grain plucking was on the sabbath (2:23),
and the healing of the man with a withered hand took place
"again" when he entered a synagogue on the sabbath (3:1–2).
Thus even according to Mark's list, these events were separated
by some time. Where had Jesus and his followers gone in the
meantime? Where did they eat (besides at the houses of friendly
toll collectors)? Where did they sleep?

Mark's arrangement of the five conflict stories is Mark's.
The events did not actually take place in such a rapid sequence. Moreover, Matthew breaks these stories up: the first
three appear in Matt 9:1–17; the last two, in Matt 12:1–14. Mark's
arrangement is more powerful dramatically, and we should
credit either Mark or a predecessor with arranging the material in such an effective way. Matthew had other interests. In
chapters 8 and 9 he collected ten miracle stories, breaking them
up a little with a few other passages. In his arrangement, the
healing of the paralytic is miracle number seven (it is the first
of the five conflict passages in Mark). After using this passage,
Matthew then added the next two passages from Mark 2, completed his list of ten healings, and saved Mark's fourth and fifth
passages for a later occasion.

Just as Mark's arrangement is Mark's, Matthew's is Matthew's. We do not know what happened when. Our uncertainty
about the contexts in which these events took place goes beyond the point where Matthew diverges from Mark. We are

Arrangement of Stories in Matthew and Mark

	Mark	Matthew
Six miracle stories		Matthew 8
Healing of paralytic	Mark 2:1–12	Matt 9:1–8
Toll gatherer	Mark 2:13–17	Matt 9:9–13
Fasting	Mark 2:18–22	Matt 9:14–17
Three more miracles		Matt 9:18–34
Instructions to the disciples		Matthew 10
Further teaching		Matthew 11
Grain on sabbath	Mark 2:23–28	Matt 12:1–8
Withered hand	Mark 3:1–6	Matt 12:9–14

first of all uncertain about the rapid-fire sequence, partly because it is intrinsically improbable, partly because Matthew does not have it. But then we note that both authors arranged their works as they wished, and we become generally uncertain about all aspects of their arrangements. Moreover, many agreements among them — for example, that these events took place in the same sequence, even if not one right after another — are explained by the fact that Matthew (and Luke) copied Mark. We do not know *for sure* how these stories related to one another, when they happened in Jesus' career, or what their precise circumstances were.

I wish here to insert a digression in order to place my discussion within its context. I am not discussing the homiletical usefulness of these stories. I can imagine a sermon that takes advantage of Mark's arrangement in order to emphasize conflict between "the establishment" and a charismatic leader. Equally I can imagine a sermon constructed around Matthew's sequence of ten miracles. Historical analysis does not destroy texts. Historians will pass away, the canonical text is still there, and modern people will wish to draw modern conclusions from it. This is perfectly valid. I think that it would be useful if *occasionally* preachers explained something about historical and critical problems in the Gospels, but there is no reason for them not to exploit the possibilities that various biblical texts offer them.

I am also not discussing whether or not the passages are *true*. Some people today have an extremely narrow and shallow definition of "truth:" it is precise narration of events. This is the model that we employ in evaluating news stories, and many of us regard it as the only model. If we hold fast to this shallow definition, we are bound to lose confidence in the Gospels entirely *since there are so many disagreements among them.* It is simply not possible for the five passages listed above to have occurred where both Matthew and Mark place them, since they do not agree. And the disagreement here is very minor compared to many of the disagreements from Gospel to Gospel. If truth is a precise narration of events, then the Gospels are not true, since they disagree in narrating the events of Jesus' life. And in this case, Christianity is not true since it rests in part on the Gospels. I am employing here *reductio ad absurdum* — reduction to the point of absurdity — to show the error of thinking that truth is precise narration of events. Truth is much broader and deeper than that, as *everyone knew prior to the nineteenth century.* Modern Fundamentalism assumes a shallow version of nineteenth-century historicism. Careful readers have always known that the Gospels disagree with one another in numerous ways, and this has not kept them from believing in their essential truth.

My own context in discussing the Gospels is that I am a historian. I want to know whatever we can know about the events of Jesus' lifetime, and in this endeavor I use the Gospels. I do not regard them as historically worthless. Nevertheless, in decades of study, I have found numerous difficulties (as have all scholars). Here I am trying to explain what is difficult about the quest for the historical Jesus, not what is true or false about Christianity. Christianity fundamentally rests on views about *what God was up to in the life of Jesus and how he understood Jesus' life and especially his death:* he sent Jesus to be the Savior of the world, and he counts Jesus' death as full atonement for the sins of the world. The historian, as historian, cannot evaluate these claims at all. That is why the disagreements among the Gospels did not trouble the many great Christians who noticed them, such as Irenaeus (second century), Eusebius (fourth century), and Luther (sixteenth century). These careful readers were not dismayed by disagreements among the Gospels since they did not equate truth with precise narration of events.

The disagreements disconcert only people who hold a shallow nineteenth-century view of truth.

We now return to the subject, which is how deficient the Gospels are as biographies of Jesus. Most readers of the Gospels do not see how uncircumstantial the stories are because there have been more than nineteen hundred years to invent circumstances: the Pharisees demanded strict obedience to their rules; they established patrols throughout Galilee; they watched charismatic healers; they were vicious and malicious; etc. But the Gospels actually do not give circumstances and motives (nor do other sources support the description of the Pharisees just given). The Gospels are composed of snippets, that have been moved here and there. I shall come back to the fact that Christians moved the small units of material from one setting to another (see p. 49). Just now I want to give an illustration to show how deficient our knowledge is when we do not know the context, that is, the circumstances in which something took place.

The most famous biographer of the ancient world was Plutarch, who wrote a series of lives of famous Greeks and Romans. Since he was writing about men who had lived very public lives, he often gave the precise circumstances in which events took place. Sometimes, however, he seems to have had only a clever saying or a striking deed, without knowing what had inspired it. We see this, for example, in his *Life of Phocion,* an account of a political and military leader in Athens in the fourth century B.C.E. In some of the chapters on Phocion's life, Plutarch simply put several short passages together one after the other. For example,

> When [Phocion] was addressing the assembly and the people refused to take his advice or even to give him a hearing, he told them, "You can make me act against my wishes, but you shall never make me speak against my judgement." (chap. 8, below the middle)[4]

This is 100 percent of the surviving evidence about this event and the concluding saying.

It will be helpful to think what we would know about Phocion if all we had were a hundred or so such passages.

We would discover that he was a public leader, that he was sometimes at odds with the majority, that he prized his intellectual independence, etc. But this understanding would be partial if we did not know on what topics he took an independent stance. If we cared as much about Phocion as we do about Jesus, a tradition would have arisen to give point and meaning to this story. It may have been that the actual debate in the Athenian assembly that day was where to dump the city's rubbish, but we would invent an important occasion: for example, we might imagine that it had to do with whether or not Athens should declare war on Sparta or send a delegation to negotiate with Persia. The significance of the saying depends on the circumstances, as Plutarch knew. But, still, he would put in a passage without context if he did not know the context, and he has a string of such passages in chapter 8 of his *Life of Phocion*. This is the way ancient writers composed material if they had inadequate knowledge of the actual close context.

The synoptic Gospels read very much like the eighth chapter of Plutarch's *Life of Phocion*. Or, rather, *most* of the chapters in the Synoptics read like this chapter from Plutarch. The story of Jesus' last week is different, and it also serves to show how little we know about the rest of Jesus' career. In my New Testament, the Gospel of Mark takes up 52 pages. Of these, the last week of Jesus' life receives 18 ½, which is 35.5 percent. I am sure that this week was unusually full, but nevertheless it is remarkable that one week gets more than a third of Mark's story of Jesus. For example, if the reader compares Mark 11–16 with Mark 1–3, he or she will note the dissimilarity in the amount of detail. In the Passion narrative, one finds a lot of circumstantial detail, and consequently we can understand that last week in Jerusalem better than the previous months or years in Galilee. On the whole, then, when we try to reconstruct the life of Jesus, except for the last week, we suffer from the lack of a coherent full narrative that explains what was going on around him when he did this or that. To repeat this first main point: we do not have an eyewitness account of Jesus' career that reliably connects words and deeds to specific occasions.

No Immediate Context

My second observation about what we lack is really just an elaboration of the first. We do not have the original immediate context of each individual unit of material. This is so because the units often lack any description of the occasion (as we have just seen). But we have also seen that the individual units were moved around to fit the needs of the person who quoted them. Many passages — not just the ones cited above — appear in different places in the three synoptic Gospels. We (that is, New Testament scholars) think that if Matthew and Luke moved Mark's passages around — which they did — Christian storytellers had been moving individual units around for some time. We cannot be confident that we ever have the original context of a given passage. Even if we had no doubts about the authenticity of the various isolated passages, the loss of the original context would be a devastating one. I shall return to the loss of context in just a minute, after pointing out the third thing that we lack.

No Certainty Regarding Origin of Sayings

That third thing is, of course, secure knowledge of which parts of the Gospels go back to the historical Jesus and which bits arose later, whether because of sayings by the heavenly Lord, prophecies by Christian speakers who were filled with the Spirit, novelistic elaborations by early Christian teachers and preachers, inadvertent changes in the course of transmission, or other factors.[5]

These are very large problems. It is my own opinion that the study of the synoptic Gospels is one of the hardest topics in the humanities. These three short books are more difficult than *Beowulf,* Chaucer, Shakespeare, or the Crusades.

These three deficiencies do not ever disappear. We can work on them and work with them in order to produce historical results that are better than mere guesses, but we can never know as much about Jesus as we know about Julius Caesar. The sources simply do not permit it. I shall, however, mention two partial solutions to our manifold problems.

Partial Solutions

Tests for Authenticity

The first is that the sayings of Jesus can be tested for authenticity. This is not the place to review the history of criteria for establishing authenticity in New Testament scholarship.[6] I shall instead mention just the two tests that I myself find most useful (*a* and *b*) and then point out the weaknesses of these tests (*c*).

a. The first criterion is multiple attestation. The strongest form of multiple attestation is seen in the passage on divorce, which I mentioned briefly above. The saying on divorce appears in the New Testament five times, and there are two principal forms of it, a short form and a long form. Both forms appear in Matthew, in two different contexts. The long form also appears in Mark, and the short form also appears in Luke and Paul (the passages are listed in n. 3). There are several variations in each of the two main forms. Paul's short version is sufficiently distinctive that we might say that there are three forms of the saying, not two. This indicates that different strands of tradition, or different schools of Christian teachers, knew *a* saying about divorce, and this diversity makes it likely that the original source is early — and is probably Jesus himself.

The passage on divorce is the *best attested* saying that is attributed to Jesus. If the reader takes several minutes to study the five passages side by side, questions will immediately arise. Did Jesus say similar things on two or three different occasions? What precisely did he say? Was he principally concerned to prohibit divorce, or was he most concerned with remarriage after divorce? The five passages are somewhat different, but despite this problem and the unanswerable questions, I feel perfectly confident that Jesus said something negative about divorce. He probably intended to forbid it, and he certainly wanted to prohibit remarriage after divorce. However, I would *not* say that this is the most important thing that we know about the teaching of Jesus. It is simply the best attested. I should add another digression to clarify my view.

I am not discussing what Christians today should believe or what marriage rules they should follow. Jesus was an ethical radical, and several of his teachings have been modified in the course of the last 1,970 years. The saying on divorce immediately ran into problems, as we see elsewhere in the New Testament. Paul advised his converts in Corinth not to contest the issue if an unbelieving partner wished to separate (1 Cor 7:15). According to Matt 19:10, Jesus' disciples thought that if divorce was not permitted, it was better never to marry. Many will find here the words of experience! The increase in annulments by the Roman Catholic Church also shows how difficult the demand is. Whatever the past and present problems created by the passages on divorce and remarriage, I am not prescribing a rule, nor do I wish to recommend that people ignore Jesus' prohibition. I wish only to describe the search for what Jesus actually said.

The second and third best-attested passages are Jesus' words over the bread and wine at the Last Supper[7] and his prediction that the Son of man would soon come from heaven.[8] All three are attributed to Jesus in Paul's letters,[9] and all three appear in the Gospels in more than one form. This is the test of "multiple attestation:" a passage appears in various sources and in various forms.

b. The second test of authenticity is this: Passages that are "against the grain" of the Gospels are good candidates for inclusion in a list of authentic passages.[10] All the Gospel writers had their own preferences, but they nevertheless included material that did not entirely agree with those preferences. This material may have been too firmly embedded in the traditions about Jesus to be jettisoned. For our example, we turn to material about John the Baptist. Jesus got his start under John, which the early Christians found a little embarrassing since it might lead to the view that John was superior to Jesus. The Gospels of Matthew and John took steps to exclude this possibility. I shall deal only with Matthew. According to this Gospel, John the Baptist predicted that someone more powerful than he would soon appear (3:11). When Jesus came to be baptized, John "would have prevented him, saying, 'I need to be baptized by you, and do you come to me?' " Jesus told him to go ahead anyway, and John baptized him (3:13–15). This exchange, including John's protest, is not in Mark or Luke, and we may take it to reveal a special concern of Matthew. He wanted to show that John acknowledged Jesus' superiority. Now we move to a later passage in Matthew. When the Baptist was in prison, he sent his disciples to Jesus with a question, "Are you the one who is to come, or are we to wait for another?" (11:2f., NRSV). It is against the grain in Matthew for the Baptist to ask this question since he had already signaled his acceptance of Jesus as the one who was to come. Therefore this question, "Are you the one?" goes into the list of probably authentic passages. Matthew did not entirely agree with it, but he included it anyway.

We can add to this the prediction of the coming of the Son of man (the passages are listed in n. 8). This prediction appears not only twice in Matthew, twice in Mark, and once in Paul, but also twice in Luke, though Luke did not like eschatology very much. (*Eschatology* is discussion or expectation of the end: the Son of man will come on clouds of heaven and gather the elect, etc.).[11] The Gospel of Luke has much less eschatology than the Gospels of Mark and Matthew, and the same author included very little eschatology in his second volume, the Acts of the Apostles. In Acts, for example, Paul does not have an eschatological message, though the Paul who wrote the letters most definitely had one. That is, Luke sometimes excised eschatology. Nevertheless, he included the prediction that the Son of man will come on a cloud (21:27). That is against the grain in Luke, and it helps to support the authenticity of the passage (which was already supported by multiple attestation).

I have offered only two criteria and a small handful of examples. More are readily available (see n. 6 above), but here I have aimed at demonstrating the process rather than at cataloguing the passages that tests for authenticity make available. The technique is basically simple, though the establishment of worthwhile criteria takes a good deal of scholarly effort.[12] Once we have criteria, we apply them to the material in the Gospels. At the end, the investigator has a pile of the passages that are probably "authentic Jesus-material." This means that they probably go back to Jesus. Uncertainty does not end here, however, since we still do not know what precise words were spoken by Jesus. I am as certain as I can be that the passage on divorce originated with Jesus, but the five forms are somewhat different. We can be sure that he opposed divorce and even surer that he was against remarriage after divorce, but we remain uncertain about precisely what he said. A study of the words of institution at the Last Supper (n. 7 above) or of the Lord's Prayer (Matt 6:9–15; Mark 11:25; Luke 11:2–4) has similar results: the main thrust is clear, but the wording varies.

c. I believe in this kind of study. I have spent years at it, and I think that it gives some good results. But it has two drawbacks. The first is that it remains highly subjective. Subjectivity cannot be avoided in anything that we do; as far as I can tell, it is simply part and parcel of life. No two of us see things in precisely the same way. I also think, however, that scholars should strive for objectivity. In the humanities in the United States today, subjectivity is, in my view, embraced far too enthusiastically. The way academic study is supposed to work is this: each scholar aims at objectivity, and the various scholars exchange their results by publishing them. The exchange is crucial since it exposes each scholar's biases, preferences, and weaknesses. Once these are assessed, progress is possible. This model is now rejected in many areas in our universities in favor of openly confessed preferences and "readings" of material, which are viewed as not open to debate because they are admitted to be completely subjective. I regret this, and I plug along, trying to be objective, and doubtless often failing. In any case, *criteriology* (as we may call it) is a subjective enterprise, even when we strive for objectivity. I regard this kind of analysis as a necessary but relatively small step towards understanding the historical Jesus.

The second weakness in this sifting of passages is that even if we could get a list or pile of passages that all scholars agreed were authentic, we would still need to put them together in some overall frame of reference — that is, in a context — for them to have much meaning.[13] For our brains, context is not an option. If we do not know the original context of an event, our clever brains will make one up. When we considered Phocion above, I pointed out that to understand fully his statement that no one could force him to have a certain opinion, we would need to know what the subject was. We can all take the concept — Phocion had "a mind of his own" — and apply it where we wish, but what was the actual application in this case? Did he say this in all possible cases or only in some?

Let me take a well-known passage from the Gospels as an illustration of the need for context. I think it likely that Jesus said the following words. The question is, What did he mean? That is, to what situation did he address himself?

> "Therefore I tell you, do not be anxious about your life, what you shall eat or what you shall drink, nor about your body, what you shall put on. Is not life more than food, and the body more than clothing? Look at the birds of the air: they neither sow nor reap nor gather into barns, and yet your heavenly Father feeds them. Are you not of more value than they? And which of you by being anxious can add one cubit to his span of life? And why are you anxious about clothing? Consider the lilies of the field, how they grow; they neither toil nor spin; yet I tell you, even Solomon in all his glory was not arrayed like one of these. But if God so clothes the grass of the field, which today is alive and tomorrow is thrown into the oven, will he not much more clothe you, O men of little faith? Therefore do not be anxious, saying, 'What shall we eat?' or 'What shall we drink?' or 'What shall we wear?' For the Gentiles seek all these things; and your heavenly Father knows that you need them all. But seek first his kingdom and his righteousness, and all these things shall be yours as well." (Matt 6:25–33, RSV)

Gerd Theissen applies this saying to Jesus' close followers ("the earliest Christian wandering charismatics") and interprets it as a statement about "the harshness of the free existence of the wandering charismatics, without homes and without protection, traveling through the country with no possessions and no occupation."[14] Richard Horsley relates the saying to "the perpetually marginal situation of the peasantry." "The point of Jesus' wisdom here was to address the intense and justifiable anxiety about *simple survival* that haunted many ordinary people."[15] Seán Freyne, who (quite correctly) has a more optimistic view of economic life in Galilee than does Horsley, suggested that perhaps "the concern[s] of Jesus' audience with food and raiment are not symptoms of a peasantry totally denuded, but rather reflect attitudes and values that the gospels generally associate with the relatively affluent."[16] It is, after all, the prosperous who spend the most time worrying about their clothes. The truth is that we do not know the original application of the saying. I wish especially to emphasize that we do not know that it addressed the economic condition of Galilean peasants in general; Jesus could have had in mind only the particular people gathered that day or, as Theissen suggested, only his disciples. Or maybe it was merely his reflection on his hosts of the previous evening, who may have been excessively materialistic. We just do not know.

I think that the precise meaning of many of the sayings will always elude us. As I indicated above, homiletically they can be usefully applied to contemporary situations. But we cannot recover the original audience or the original immediate circumstances, and thus we cannot know precisely what Jesus had in mind when he uttered each of his memorable sayings.

We have thus far considered the difficulties of finding out about Jesus and one way of overcoming at least some of them: tests for authenticity. Consideration of these tests revealed that what we really need is context. But we do not have the original contexts of the various passages in the Gospels — or, if we have them, we cannot be sure of them. It follows of course that the second way of replying to our difficulties is to find a helpful context that is secure.

Understanding the Larger Context

We can do something positive about contexts that are somewhat larger than the immediate occasions of Jesus' sayings. Contexts come in all shapes and sizes. Each of us has a personal context that is not quite the same as that of anyone else. We all share larger contexts with many people (our families, fellow employees, and the like). And all humans now alive share a very large context: the closing years of the twentieth century. While we cannot know the immediate context of many of Jesus' sayings and deeds, we can know larger contexts. We can, for example, study and describe first-century Jewish Palestine, and if we do this, we shall understand Jesus better. This particular activity has occupied more of my life than any other endeavor,[17] and in my opinion it does not occupy nearly enough of the time of most New Testament scholars. Nevertheless I cannot here launch into a thousand-page review of Jewish Palestine in Jesus' day. There is another context that we can discover and that I can briefly describe: the context of Jesus' career — how he got his start and what happened in his movement after his death and Resurrection.

As we noted above, Jesus started his career by being baptized by John the Baptist. John was an eschatological prophet: that is, he thought that God was about to intervene in the world and change it.[18] He called people to repent, and he warned that "the ax is lying at the root of the trees" (Matt 3:10, NRSV).

Now we move to the earliest evidence about the Christian movement after Jesus' death and Resurrection. The oldest surviving Christian document is 1 Thessalonians, which is the earliest of Paul's letters. In 1 Thess 1:9–10, Paul writes to his converts that they had turned to God from idols and were awaiting God's Son from heaven. It appears, quite surprisingly, that Paul had not originally taught his converts in Thessalonica to expect death and Resurrection. They expected Christ to come from heaven while they were still alive, and they were surprised when some of their members died. Paul wrote to reassure them by saying that the dead in Christ would rise first and would not miss out on the new age:

> For this we declare to you by the word of the Lord, that we who are alive, who are left until the coming of the Lord, will by no means precede those who have died. For the Lord himself, with a cry of command, with the archangel's call and with the sound of God's trumpet, will descend from heaven, and the dead in Christ will rise first. Then we who are alive, who are left, will be caught up in the clouds together with them to meet the Lord

in the air; and so we will be with the Lord forever. (1 Thess
4:15–17)

Paul concluded the letter by praying that the Thessalonians
would be sound and blameless in spirit and soul and body
when the Lord arrived (5:23) — note, sound in body. He still
expected most of them to be alive. We know that Paul disagreed
with other Christian leaders on some topics. There is, however,
no indication that this was one of the points in dispute. The
early Christian community expected the Lord to come in the
near future.

Thus Jesus began by being baptized by an eschatological
prophet, and shortly after he was gone, his followers formed a
community that expected the climax of history in the near future. This is the context of Jesus' own career. We must fit him
in between an eschatological prophet and eschatological apostles. Surely his own message was eschatological as well. And
then we note that much of the sayings material is eschatological. Consider the Lord's Prayer and the phrase, "Your kingdom
come. Your will be done, on earth as it is in heaven" (Matt 6:10).
That is what Jesus expected: that God's kingdom would come
to earth.[19]

This, I think, helps us understand Jesus better than does
the careful sifting of individual passages. Moreover, it gives a
context within which to place the rest of the material. Jesus
thought that God would intervene directly in the world and
change it for the better. He seems also to have spent some
time describing how to live in the present as God would have
people live in the kingdom. Meekness, humility, love, and
mercy — these were the qualities that should mark the lives
of citizens of the coming kingdom of God. The original context was Jesus' view of the coming kingdom and the qualities
that were suitable to it. His sayings, fortunately, have shown
themselves able, with some help from dedicated interpreters, to
transcend the original context and to provide guidance in other
circumstances.

It is sometimes frustrating for Christian leaders to try to
derive guidelines for social improvement from the Bible. One of

the sources of this problem is this simple fact: both Jesus and Paul, who dominate the New Testament, expected God to intervene directly in the world in the near future. We have a hard time obtaining social programs from the teachings of Jesus and Paul because they did not have social programs but expected divine transformation. I have always been struck by the fact that Martin Luther King relied heavily on Gandhi for his views. He of course quoted the Bible heavily, but Gandhi's philosophy of passive resistance actually provided the framework. That philosophy, unlike the teaching of Jesus, was designed to change society. There are a lot of individual parallels between what Jesus said and what Gandhi said, but their overall outlooks were quite different. It was King's application of Gandhi's views that led to social change.

The subject assigned me was not to give an overall description of Jesus as I see him, and I have given only a few hints in this direction. I have tried, instead, to indicate why it is difficult to obtain good evidence about Jesus and some of the ways in which we may overcome the difficulties. The one difficulty that is basic to all the others is that Jesus' followers did not immediately sit down and write about their days with him in Galilee and Jerusalem. After they experienced the Resurrection, they believed that Jesus would soon return, and they tried to win others to faith in him. In doing so, they naturally used many of his sayings and deeds, but they used them to suit their own messages at the time. The result is that we do not have a good, circumstantial account of his life that ties his teaching and his deeds to the specific occasions that produced them. We do not know the *original immediate* contexts of the various passages in the Gospels, nor do we know for sure which parts of the material are "authentic," that is, which actually go back to Jesus. We can, however, ameliorate these difficulties. We can test the passages for authenticity, and we can reconstruct the *general* context of Jesus' career, which was eschatology — the coming divine transformation of the world.

Notes

1. My principal works on Jesus are these: *Jesus and Judaism* (Philadelphia: Fortress; London: SCM, 1985); with Margaret Davies, *Studying the Synoptic Gospels* (London: SCM; Philadelphia: Trinity Press International, 1989); *Jewish Law from Jesus to the Mishnah: Five Studies* (London: SCM; Philadelphia: Trinity Press International, 1990) chap. 1; *The Historical Figure of Jesus* (London: Allen Lane Penguin Press, 1993; New York: Viking Penguin, 1994); "Jesus in Historical Context," *Theology Today* 50 (1993) 429–48.

2. On the dates of the Gospels, see Sanders and Davies, *Studying the Synoptic Gospels,* 5–21. There is a good deal of uncertainty about dates, and some people date the Gospels earlier than do I. Similarly, some place Jesus' death a little earlier than 30, while some prefer one or two years later. We also cannot date the deaths of the first apostles very accurately. James the brother of John was executed during the reign of Herod Agrippa I, therefore 41–44 C.E. Paul and Peter were probably both martyred in the early to mid-60s. We do not have good information about when the other original apostles died. Those who wish to look into dates more thoroughly may consult the principal biblical dictionaries, which have articles on "Chronology" and brief bibliographies. I discussed the chronology of Jesus' life in *Historical Figure of Jesus,* 11–12 (birth), 282–90 (death).

3. On divorce, see Matt 5:31–32; 19:3–12; Mark 10:2–12; Luke 16:18; 1 Cor 7:10. One context appears in Mark (paralleled in Matthew 19), one in Matthew 5, and a third in Luke 16.

4. *Plutarch: The Age of Alexander,* trans. Ian Scott-Kilvert (Harmondsworth: Penguin; New York: Viking Penguin, 1973, repr. 1983).

5. We should especially note that some stories about Jesus might be derived from the Hebrew Bible (the "Old Testament"). For example, Luke 7:11–17, the story of the son of the widow of Nain, is similar to stories about Elijah (1 Kgs 17:17–24) and Elisha (2 Kgs 4:25b–37). Such suggestions can never be decisively proved, but it would have been fairly simple for a Christian preacher or teacher to think that Elijah and Elisha were forerunners of Jesus and that therefore their miracles foreshadowed his. If their miracles foreshadowed his, then he performed miracles similar to theirs. Thus the theological view of "foreshadowing" (or fulfillment of Scripture) could have led to the creation of one or more miracle stories.

6. For a fuller account, see Sanders and Davies, *Studying the Synoptic Gospels,* chaps. 20–21.

7. The Lord's Supper: Matt 26:26–29; Mark 14:22–25; Luke 22:15–20; 1 Cor 11:23–25.

8. The Son of man will come: Matt 16:27–28; Mark 8:38–9:1;

Luke 9:26–27; Matt 24:30–31; Mark 13:26–27; Luke 21:27–28; 1 Thess 4:15–17.

9. In the case of the passage on the arrival of the Son of man, Paul refers to the "return" of "the Lord" instead of the "coming" of the "Son of man." This reveals that he and probably others had interpreted the "Son of man" in the teaching of Jesus as a reference to himself.

10. This criterion should not be converted into a negative test; that is, I would not argue that passages that are "with the grain" are inauthentic. The Gospel writers must have held views that corresponded to things that Jesus actually said and did, and my own assumption is that there are many such cases. It is nevertheless useful to know which passages are "against the grain," since these are passages that the authors of the Gospels might have wished to excise or modify but did not, presumably because they were too well established in the tradition.

11. The word "eschatology" is somewhat misleading since the early Christians did not expect the universe to come to an immediate end. According to Paul, Christ would return to the earth and reign until he defeated all his enemies; the end would come only after the defeat of Death, the last enemy (1 Cor 15:23–26). For this view in the Gospels, see *Historical Figure of Jesus*, 93–96, 174, 181–84.

12. My criterion called "against the grain" is intended to replace the criterion of "dissimilarity" or "double dissimilarity," especially as the latter has usually been applied. The "criterion of dissimilarity" was this: material attributed to Jesus that was dissimilar to later Christian theology was authentic; material that agreed was inauthentic. "Double dissimilarity" meant that material that was either like Christian theology or like Judaism should be rejected. There are three reasons for not applying these rules. (1) These criteria were biased in favor of uniqueness, which meant that they resulted in a Jesus who was isolated both from the society in which he lived and the Church that grew up after his death and resurrection. (2) It is intrinsically probable that Jesus agreed with his contemporaries on many issues (as in Mark 12:28–34) and that his followers agreed with him. (3) "Judaism" and "Christian theology" are large and flexible entities, about which we know many things; on the other hand, we are a long way from knowing everything about them. It is difficult to know what is "dissimilar" to both Judaism and the early Church. Thus these categories are too big and too uncertain to use. My substitute, "against the grain," fixes on only one or more of our Gospels, which are much more manageable than "Christian theology," and also I seldom apply it negatively (n. 10 above). For the early history of the test of dissimilarity and double dissimilarity, see Rudolf Bultmann, *The History*

of the Synoptic Tradition, trans. John Marsh, rev. ed. (Oxford: Blackwell, 1968) 205; Norman Perrin, *Rediscovering the Teaching of Jesus,* New Testament Library (London: SCM; New York: Harper and Row, 1967) 39–43. For critical discussion, see Morna Hooker, "Christology and Methodology," *NTS* 17 (1970–71) 480–87; D. G. A. Calvert, "An Examination of the Criteria for Distinguishing the Authentic Words of Jesus," *NTS* 18 (1971–72) 209–19.

13. Cf. R. S. Barbour, *Traditio-Historical Criticism of the Gospels* (London: SPCK, 1972) 18; Bruce Chilton, *God in Strength: Jesus' Announcement of the Kingdom* (Freistadt: F. Plöchl, 1979) 20.

14. Gerd Theissen, *Sociology of Early Palestinian Christianity,* English Translation (Philadelphia: Fortress, 1978) 12–14.

15. Richard A. Horsley, *Jesus and the Spiral of Violence: Popular Jewish Resistance in Roman Palestine* (San Francisco: Harper, 1987) 256f., emphasis mine.

16. Seán Freyne, *Galilee, Jesus, and the Gospels: Literary Approaches and Historical Investigations* (Philadelphia: Fortress, 1988) 166.

17. See my *Paul and Palestinian Judaism: A Comparison of Patterns of Religion* (London: SCM; Philadelphia: Fortress, 1977); *Jesus and Judaism; Jewish Law from Jesus to the Mishnah; Judaism: Practice and Belief 63* B.C.E.–*70 C.E.* (London: SCM; Philadelphia: Trinity Press International, 1992).

18. On eschatology, see n. 11 above.

19. To continue the discussion of "dissimilarity" (above, n. 12), I should note that I am arguing that here there was continuity from John to Jesus to the apostles. The criterion of "double dissimilarity," if rigidly applied, would destroy our ability to discover the context of Jesus' life and work. We would have to dismiss the letters of Paul and also first-century Jewish Palestine as irrelevant, since we would imagine that Jesus was completely unique, that is, contextless. This is the antithesis of historical research.

Chapter 3

The Word Becomes Flesh: Jesus, Gender, and Sexuality

Amy-Jill Levine

In the initial planning both for Florida Southern's 1998 Biblical Symposium and for the published proceedings of that gathering, I was asked to address the question, What do we get when investigating the historical Jesus in a historically informed way? I knew I would be sharing the podium and these pages with Professors James H. Charlesworth, John Dominic Crossan, and E. P. Sanders; I also knew that composing an essay that would substantively, comprehensively, and equitably summarize my colleagues' methods and emphases would likely be impossible. The path to the answer of What do we get? was already riddled with stumbling blocks.

My problem encompassed more than the technical difficulties of epitomizing complex approaches and subtle conclusions.

My gratitude to Nashville's Hillsboro Presbyterian Church and to the priests of the Roman Catholic Diocese of Middle Tennessee for their thoughtful questions and trenchant suggestions on earlier versions of this essay in its oral form. For elaboration on the themes in this paper, with particular attention to the divorce sayings and anti-Jewish interpretations, see Amy-Jill Levine, "Jesus, Gender, and Sexuality: A Jewish Critique," in Klutznick Symposium Collection, ed. L. Greenspoon (forthcoming).

I can reconstruct my colleague's views from their publications, my notes on their talks, reviews by others, and in the cases of Crossan and Charlesworth, from long-standing personal friendships, but the pictures I develop may not be, at least to my colleagues' self-perceptions, accurate. I risk emphasizing the wrong issues, misquoting statements or taking them out of context, and otherwise distorting their positions. I may even find myself unconsciously adapting their material to fit my own ideological perspectives or what I perceive to be the interests of my audience. Even if I cite directly from their books and articles, problems continue. First, scholars sometimes modify their views as they refine their methods, respond to critics, and find new evidence. Consequently, any summary risks obsolescence. Second, even the most careful editors make mistakes. For example, the program distributed to the participants at Florida Southern's Biblical Symposium contained errors about my publications (my next book is forthcoming from Harvard, not Cambridge) and my editorial work (for the *Journal of Biblical Studies*, not the *Journal of Biblical Literature*); whether error or not, my children say that the publicity photograph in the program does not even look like me.

If it is difficult to locate with full confidence the historical Crossan, Sanders, Charlesworth, or even Levine, then *Qal v'homer*,[1] how much more so is it difficult to locate the historical Jesus? How much trustworthiness should we grant the Gospels, written after the crucifixion, not by eyewitnesses, and in Greek rather than Aramaic?

I think we should grant them a great deal. While the specifics of the symposium program were incorrect, overall the impression given of me — of a writer and teacher who is interested in gender roles on the one hand and the relationship between Church and Synagogue on the other and who usually smiles — was correct. Similarly, while the words and deeds the Gospels attribute to Jesus have been modified, edited, and expanded by the Evangelists to fit the needs of the developing Church, I think much of their general depiction of Jesus' words and deeds has good claims to credibility.

Finally, since my editors have no desire for a monograph, I

cannot give a comprehensive picture of the Jesus who emerges from the application of various methods, let alone offer critiques or develop pastoral implications. For manageability, and given my particular interests, I shall focus on two interrelated categories often absent from studies of the historical Jesus: gender and sexuality. Our understanding of these issues in turn may contribute to our views of matters pressing in today's political climate: attitudes towards marriage and divorce, procreation, and male/female relationships.

The timeliness of these issues and their absence from much of what has come to be known as the "third quest of the historical Jesus" are not the only reasons I have for my focus. At Vanderbilt's Divinity School, I serve as the director of the Carpenter Program in Religion, Gender, and Sexuality, whose mandate is to encourage education and communication on these controversial topics.[2] In this capacity, I get a number of phone calls and letters. Here are three examples (paraphrased slightly):

1. "When all those Jews were thanking God for not making them women, slaves, or gentiles, Jesus was talking with women, healing them, encouraging them. The Church has sunk back into Paul's Rabbinic Judaism rather than followed Jesus' break with patriarchy."

2. "I got pregnant when I was in junior high and had to get married. My husband never loved me. He beat me, and when he got tired of that, he moved out. We haven't been together for over two years. I've become a Christian, and in church I met a man I love. My pastor says I can't get divorced, and if I remarry, I'll be committing adultery. What would Jesus say?"

3. "The Bible is my guide for how to live, and my girlfriend and I often study it together. Everything was fine until we started making wedding plans, and we checked to see what Jesus says about marriage. I'm not sure I like what I've found. Jesus wasn't married, he praised 'eunuchs for the kingdom of Heaven' (Matthew 19), and he told husbands to leave their wives and follow him. Now I'm

thinking of calling off the wedding, or at least telling my fiancée that we shouldn't have sex. She thinks I'm nuts. What do you think?"

Engagement

Responses to such questions should address not only the content of Jesus' teaching but also the rationale. Pronouncement is often insufficient apart from explanation; as the mother of two children, I am well aware that the reply "Because I said so" is unhelpful for developing moral responsibility or religious commitment. This extension is necessary even for those who claim, "If the Bible says it, I believe it." The most literal of readers needs to judge whether a statement is imperative, ideal, metaphor, even sarcasm; whether it applies to both men and women, to only one group or an individual, to all people for all times.

The question *why* greatly occupies those engaged in historical Jesus research: whether we see Jesus as expecting an apocalyptic end to the world or a new form of social organization brought about through human endeavor, as a peasant addressing social evils or a prophet seeking spiritual renewal, necessarily impacts our interpretation of his sexual ethic and his view of gender roles. However, compared with the numerous works on Jesus' parables, healings, view of *Halachah* (literally: "the way"; generally: following Torah), and the circumstances of his crucifixion, there remains little written by academic "questers" on his view of sex and gender.

Few biblical scholars before the 1970s talked about sexuality or gender at all, let alone Jesus' sexuality. Even the article titled "Sex and Sexuality" in the recent *Anchor Bible Dictionary* only considers the Hebrew Scriptures (demonstrating thereby to the literalist that there is no sex in the New Testament).[3] On sexual ethics, Paul was and remains the more frequently evoked; this is appropriate since he has more to say on the topic. Still others did not find the issues relevant. Noting that Jesus had a message for all people, they saw little reason to concentrate on his message to or relationships with women.

Another contingent may have been discouraged by the Evangelists' lack of sustained detail on women's roles. The Gospel accounts of women and discussions of sexuality are, to use J. Cheryl Exum's term, "fragmented."[4] Whereas the stories of Jesus, and to a great extent of the disciples and even the Pharisees, develop from scene to scene, women lack a progressive story line; like guest stars on a television show, they appear, make a noteworthy contribution, and then vanish. Topics concerning sexuality, such as marriage, family structures, divorce, celibacy, and procreation, occur sporadically, but they are diffused throughout the texts.

Finally, until very recently, scholars either did not find the topics of gender and sexuality of interest or, if they did, feared such study would be labeled faddish, inflammatory, or — heaven forbid — "feminist." These were not the sorts of subjects that would enhance a tenure file. Consideration of what scholars find interesting and valuable should not be passed over too quickly. Our questions, methods, and conclusions are products, implicitly or explicitly, consciously or unconsciously, of our academic contacts and cultural contexts.

Recent studies of peasant cultures and the effects of urbanization on agrarian economic and social structures inform Crossan's works. Innovative approaches to Rabbinic texts and increasing familiarity with the diversity of Second Temple Judaism underlie Sanders's studies. Placing Jesus in his Jewish context, particularly through investigation of the Pseudepigrapha and the Qumran scrolls, determines much of Charlesworth's corpus. Biblical scholars today bring literary-critical approaches to the parables, cross-cultural anthropology to Galilean village life, studies of millenarian movements and cult formation to the community Jesus called forth, etc. Moreover, many of those who study Jesus, including my three colleagues, recognize that what biblical scholars say both informs and is informed by what clergy communicate to their congregations: for example, contemporary implications of the Jesus quest have enormously high stakes for those worried about anti-Semitism and sexism.

Correspondingly, from the '70s "women's lib" to the '90s "backlash," feminists and nonfeminists — self-proclaimed and otherwise — have brought the categories of gender and sexuality to biblical studies. As increasing numbers of women find a home in pulpits and lecterns, and as various groups celebrate or condemn this presence, it is not surprising that questions of gender and sexuality are finally being asked of Jesus and the Gospels.[5]

Whether Jesus himself would have seen these questions as of interest is another matter. Difficult as it is to locate his views of *Halachah* or the temple, it is more difficult to determine his attitude toward women *as women* and harder still to conceptualize the history of the women he encountered: his followers, those he healed, those who regarded him as possessed, or those who dismissed him. Nevertheless, lack of sustained detail, clear sources, a fully viable method, and other components of the historiographical task has never been a preventative when it comes to talking about Jesus.

In popular literature, studies of Jesus, gender, and sexuality tend to be based less on rigorous historical method and less on knowledge of the primary Jewish, Christian, and pagan sources than on stereotype (e.g., Jesus was married because Jesus was a rabbi and all rabbis were married) or apologetic (Jesus didn't really mean what he said about divorce, remarriage, etc.). Worse, both stereotype and apologetics frequently lead to or are characterized by anti-Judaism.

Christian feminists seeking a supportive Jesus had little evidence of his attempt to overthrow gender bifurcation; they had no women among the Twelve; they had no call of a woman comparable to that of Peter or Matthew; they had no pronouncement such as "in me there is neither male nor female" (cf. Gal 3:28). While women may have been at the Last Supper, their presence is unrecorded (the silence of the sources may indicate either presence suppressed or absence unremarked). But these feminists did have one of the "master's tools," which they used to great effect: they focused on women the lenses ground by those supersessionist interpreters who saw Jesus overturning a Judaism categorized as obsessively concerned with legal minutiae while lacking morality, love, and compassion.[6] So, they concluded, Jesus came to correct Jewish views on women. The worse these scholars painted Jesus' Jewish context, the more feminist he looked.[7]

Correction of this view on both feminist and nonfeminist fronts has come, in great thanks to the work of E. P. Sanders. His *Paul and Palestinian Judaism* was a watershed treatment of the problems with stereotyping Second Temple Judaism as monolithic and atavistic.[8] But even in the better studies, Sanders's lessons are forgotten or ignored when the subject turns, if it turns at all, to women. For example, although N. T. Wright's magisterial *The New Testament and the Victory of God* does present brief treatments of Mary and Martha and of Jesus' pronouncements on divorce, it does not integrate gender or sexuality into its larger picture of Jesus. What Wright does say is typical of modern mainstream comments on Jesus and women. Appealing to cross-cultural anthropology and the broadly termed "social sciences" to propose a model of "a first-century Palestinian village," he interprets Luke 10:38–42 to reveal not simply that Mary is "spiritual" and Martha "practical" but to sound "a much more subversive note...Mary has refused to be confined to the women's quarters."[9] This citation seems an endorsement of my first caller: Jesus combats misogynistic Judaism.

It is true that Mary is not confined to the complex of rooms called *gynaikonitis* (women's quarters), which were not just for women but also for slaves and various domestic activities.[10] True, Jesus has praise for Mary, who sits at his feet. Martha, needing help — probably in food preparation — and seeking Mary's aid, he rebukes. But I still find Wright's reading wrong. For example, why assume that the house had women's quarters? Where are archaeological reports of Judean villages and analyses of social class? Only the very wealthy had the luxury of such separate quarters; further, were Martha this well-off, surely she would have had a wealth of household help. On the other hand, why assume that upper-class women, in *gynaikonitis*, were confined within their own homes? Where is classical history and cross-cultural analysis of gender-bifurcated societies? Given the active manner in which she is portrayed, who would have confined Martha? Indeed, who would have dared? The only other family member Luke mentions is her sister, Mary. Even in John's narrative, which identifies her brother as Lazarus, there is still no indication either that someone is constraining Martha or that her actions, including those at Lazarus's tomb, are anomalous. Finally, the house belongs to Martha (Luke 10:38); classical and Rabbinic sources as well as several early Christian texts too indicate women's economic independence.

To claim that Jesus, or Luke, drew Mary and Martha out of a system of separation and suppression replaces history with theology. It is as unsubtle and as apologetic as the counterclaim, based on the same story and made by those disenchanted with Christianity, that Jesus permitted women followers as long as they remained silent, servile, and sitting at his feet.

When we reconstruct Second Temple social history by looking at Jewish Law from Jesus to the Mishnah or at Judaism's practice and beliefs, from say 63 B.C.E. (Pompey's entry into Jerusalem) until 70 C.E. (the destruction of the Second Temple),[11] when we search the Dead Sea Scrolls and the Pseudepigrapha to locate Jesus within Judaism,[12] and when we broaden our historical focus to include the Mediterranean world and peasant life,[13] we find a Galilee and Judea that was patriarchal and androcentric (what wasn't?). The issue, however, is one of degree. While social roles and religious responsibilities differed for men and women, Second Temple Judaism in its various forms did not epitomize misogynism. The Rabbinic materials should not be selectively chosen, retrojected back to pre-70 Jewish practice, and read therein as descriptive rather than prescriptive (any more than Tertullian's misogynism should be attributed to Jesus). To learn anything about Jesus' attitude toward women, let alone gender roles and human sexuality, we cannot begin by stacking the deck against Second Temple Judaism.

The Gospels in fact appear to counter this view of Jewish repression. They find quite unremarkable women's public presence (Mark 5:24–34; 12:42; Luke 7:11–15; 8:1–3; 11:27; etc.); they present no indication of a society obsessed with laws of family purity.[14] These impressions are confirmed by sources as varied as Josephus and Philo, the Apocrypha, the Pseudepigrapha, papyrus collections, a substantial bulk of Rabbinic writings, etc.[15]

Conversely, the Gospels offer no evidence that Jesus questioned what has come to be called the "sexual division of labor." The parables and sayings reflect traditional gender roles: the woman who seeks the lost coin in her house is paired with the shepherd in the field; the woman who puts yeast into dough matches the man who plants the mustard seed. The women grind meal; the men recline on the dining couch (Luke 17:35) or, in Matthew's version, work in the field. Even the birds of the air and the lilies of the field may be gendered images. In turn, no women in the Gospels explicitly seek to escape the demands of the so-called "oppressive patriarchal family."

Much of what Jesus said and did, as best as I can reconstruct his message and mission, had revolutionary potential: mandates like forgiving all debts, giving without expectation of return, thinking less about social convention and personal honor, resisting oppression without resorting to violence, basing identity on deed rather than family name or economic assets. But I cannot agree with my first caller who would accept Crossan's claim that the "Sophia-Christ" drew forth a "radically egalitarian [kingdom that] rendered sexual and social, political and religious distinctions completely irrelevant and anachronistic."[16] Jesus did not combat androcentrism and did not seek to break down gender roles. He likely advocated celibacy, as we shall see, but it is not necessarily the case that sexual asceticism would be congenial to all women (or all men). My first caller was very well motivated, but his attempt to reform the Church by negatively categorizing early Judaism as misogynistic and positively categorizing Jesus as proactive on women's rights is both bad history and bad theology.

Marriage and Divorce

What I have so far unveiled applies directly to my second interlocutor, the young woman who wanted to remarry. I wish I had easy answers for her.

Jesus forbade both divorce and remarriage. His pronouncements are multiply attested in the canonical tradition (Mark
10:2–12; 1 Cor 7:10–11; Matt 5:31f.; 19:3–9; Luke 16:16–18; cf.
17:1–2 [Q]). Similar comments appear in the prophet Malachi
(2:13–16) and the Dead Sea Scrolls, so the legislation is not
anomalous in its cultural context.[17] There is no evidence of Jesus
or his followers being charged with encouraging divorce (as
there is, for example, with associating with prostitutes or sinners).[18] Finally, the topic of divorce was of general interest at
his time, such that it is likely someone would have asked his
opinion.

Less certain are rationale and result: why forbid divorce,
and what effect does this interdiction have on women? The answer most often given to the first question is that the proscription responds to a particular social problem: namely, Jewish
men were divorcing their wives at whim and leaving them des-
titute. Such a construct makes Jesus congenial to those groups
who want to institute covenantal marriage, restrict divorce, and
otherwise legislate "family values" given what they perceive to
be an increasingly decadent society. This approach, once again,
relies on a derogatory stereotype in order to explain Jesus'
radical demand.[19]

Ironically, this convention categorizes Second Temple Judaism, not as a retrograde Puritanism in which women are
confined to their quarters, but as a sexual hedonism in which
women are cast out into the street. Like that other stereotype,
however, it is not well supported by the sources. First, we have
no evidence that divorce was rampant in the period. The primary support for this view is the statement attributed to Rabbi
Akiva (d. 135 C.E.) that a husband can divorce for any reason, such as his finding a woman prettier than his wife.[20] This
is Rabbinic rhetoric demonstrating what is possible given certain legal presuppositions. It is no more descriptive of Second
Temple Jewish life than Jesus' exhortations to pluck out the offending eye and chop off the offending hand are indicative of a
first-century group of blind and maimed messianists.[21]

Second, Jewish women received marriage contracts (*Ke-
tubot*), which both made divorce prohibitive and assured them

some financial security when it did occur.[22] Referring to the early second-century marriage and divorce documents from Murabba'at and Nahal Hever, John Collins remarks: "Both types of contract...are concerned for the economic well-being of the wife. This concern remains central to the well-documented development of Jewish marriage contracts in later tradition."[23] It is as historically problematic and theologically vapid to praise a command against divorce by positing a Jewish society out of moral control as it would be to suggest that Jesus' interdiction is designed to maintain relationships that begin in or disintegrate into abuse, violence, and hate.

Third, arguments against divorce and remarriage are consistent with Jesus' interest in reconfiguring the formation and role of kinship groups: "Who are my mother and my brothers? ...Whoever does the will of God" (Mark 3:33–35, NRSV). Such social planning puts Jesus at odds with most, but not all, Jews of his time.[24] The Qumran scrolls posit such a community, as do Philo's Therapeutae/Therapeutrides and several Greek philosophical schools. Like a number of these other groups as well, Jesus endorses separation from the biological kinship group. Luke 18:29–30 reads, "Truly I tell you, there is no one who has left house or wife or brothers or parents or children, for the sake of the kingdom of God, who will not get back very much more in this age, and in the age to come eternal life."[25]

If Jesus was convinced — as were Paul, the authors of several Dead Sea Scrolls, and apparently John the Baptist — that a new way of living was breaking in, then his endorsing of fictive kinship groups and countercultural views of the family should not be unexpected. This is what millenarian groups do, from Africa to Melanesia to the Shakers and the group known as Heaven's Gate. A reformist sexual ethic with strongly ascetic (or strongly libertinistic) content is often the hallmark of apocalyptic communities, as is a move toward recreating the golden age.[26] This explanation also accounts for Jesus' appeal to Adam and Eve in grounding his proscription: millenarian communities frequently associate the age to come (*Endzeit*) with the past's golden age (*Urzeit*). Jesus apparently expected, even as he attempted to create a new Eden, a setting where humanity lived at peace with nature, where ownership of property and family connections were not the ground of being. As Mark puts it:

> "Because of your hardness of heart he [Moses] wrote this commandment [concerning the opportunity of divorce] for you. But from the beginning of creation, 'God made them male and female.' 'For this reason a man shall leave his father and mother and be joined to his wife, and the two shall become one flesh.' So they are no longer two, but one flesh. Therefore what God has joined together, let no one separate." (Mark 10:5–9)

Not all the studies of Jesus subscribe to this eschatological-apocalyptic explanation. However, the other constructs are less convincing. If Jesus were a Cynic, uninterested in apocalyptic eschatology but very interested in social critique, he may have issued a prohibition against remarriage. For Cynics, marriage would be seen as demanding attention to producing heirs, toward sexual intercourse, toward the constraints that come with family life. Marriage is then the opposite of the freedom that men should have and that the Cynics sought. According to the Stoic Epictetus, the unmarried Cynic makes it his duty to comment on the morality of the marriages of others.[27] Why a Cynic would legislate the maintenance of the marital arrangement, which is clearly a cultural construct, is a more difficult question. Then again, Cynics took their name from the Greek term for "dog"; Diogenes received the epithet because of his "public defecation and immodest, public sexual behavior."[28] To press the Cynic analogy given Jesus' sexual asceticism would therefore be barking up the wrong tree.

Perhaps Jesus was a Mediterranean peasant dedicated to social justice apart from apocalyptic or millenarian considerations. In this case, he may have resisted divorce, recognizing as destructive the separation of families caused by increasing urbanization and the attendant loss of peasant land. However, this model does not help account for the commands to leave families and follow him.

Antidivorce legislation may also have been a matter of practicality. The pronouncements are less focused on spousal separation than on one of the partners remarrying: "Whoever divorces his wife and marries another commits adultery against her, and if she divorces her husband and marries another, she commits adultery" (Mark 10:11–12). Where husbands and wives are following Jesus, the last thing he and his movement need are charges of, or temptations to, adultery, nor does he, apparently, want loyalty to a spouse or the sexual availability that comes with marriage to interfere with his mission.[29] Of the various options regarding Jesus' divorce pronouncements, the apocalyptic-eschatological prophet of Jewish restoration theology provides the most convincing explanation. While the other modes can accommodate the prohibition, they do not as sufficiently account for its relationship to other pronouncements, cross-cultural parallels, and the almost immediate revision of its radicality (e.g., Paul's "if she does separate" in 1 Cor 7:11 and Matthew's *porneia* clause).[30]

Where then is our second interlocutor? I'd like to think that if she asked Jesus directly, he would tell her to follow her heart; he would tell her that in cases of abuse, divorce is not only appropriate but necessary (cf. 1 Cor 7:15). I would like to think that he would attend her second wedding — and even provide the wine. But a Jesus who provides comforting answers is, while more palatable, often less historical.

I think he would say she should call no man "lord" and remain celibate, and this because of his apocalyptic, eschatological perspective. For my conservative caller, alas, such historical contextualization was irrelevant. More helpful to her was discussion of Matthew's *porneia* clause (of which the husband was clearly guilty), appeal to John's "woman taken in adultery" (since it was the "sin of fornication" that prompted the first marriage), and the questions, "Do you think God brought together you and your first husband; did God bring together you and the man you met in church?" I also gave her the phone numbers of several local ministers. I do not know what she decided.

Consummation

Then there is my third caller, the fiancé who hears a message of celibacy. Again, the tradition is not as supportive of contemporary concerns as I would wish. That is, I think he heard correctly.

The tradition presumes Jesus is unmarried. His designation as "bridegroom" reinforces rather than compromises his virginity; it is the husband — a role Jesus does not fulfill — not the groom who consummates the relationship. And, like Jesus, the majority of his followers appear outside marital structures. The disciples speak of leaving their families to follow Jesus (e.g., Matt 19:27–29), and no spouses are listed for Martha and Mary, Mary Magdalene, or the other women from Galilee. Even the Syro-Phoenician woman (implicitly) and the Samaritan woman (explicitly) are outside marital structures. No account depicts Jesus speaking directly with a woman expressly embedded in a marriage save for Jairus's wife, present at the healing of her daughter (Mark 5:40).

The tradition also cautions against sexual desire. Matt 5:27–28 not only forbids adultery but asserts that "everyone who looks at a woman with lust has already committed adultery with her in his heart." It may caution also against self-gratification related to that desire. Mark 9:43 exhorts, "If your hand causes you to stumble, cut it off; it is better for you to enter life maimed than to have two hands and to go to hell," and Matthew juxtaposes this saying to the pronouncement on lusting (Matt 5:29). There are some Rabbinic hints of at least one tradition that advocated cutting off the hand for masturbation (cf. in a different context Deut 25:11–12),[31] and in Semitic languages, "hand" can function as a euphemism for "penis."[32]

Among the more controversial sayings attributed to Jesus are ones in Matt 19:10–12: "There are eunuchs who have been so from birth, and there are eunuchs who have been made eunuchs by others, and there are eunuchs who have made themselves eunuchs for the sake of the kingdom of heaven. Let anyone accept this who can" (v. 12). This statement has been seen as a prohibition against remarriage by widowers (although why a widower would be called a "eunuch" or how the status of widower relates to birth remains unclear) and as a call to self-castration (which is both contrary to *Halachah* and unattested in the earliest traditions). It is, however, consistent with Mark

12:18–27, which describes the ideal (resurrected) state as a celibate one where "[men] neither marry nor are [women] given in marriage" because they will be "like angels in heaven."[33] It is also consistent with Jesus' concern that followers become like little children (Mark 10:15; Matt 19:14; Luke 18:17): usually seen as representing innocence or helplessness, children are also marked by virginity and lack of sexual shame. As Crossan puts it, "a kingdom of children is a kingdom of the celibate."[34] The consistency is only slightly indirect: eunuchs could marry, and they did have sexual relationships, but they did not produce children. In a world where the dominant ethos was to have children — to preserve the family name, to inherit family property — Jesus' statement echoes his concern for humility and self-abnegation. The "eunuch for the kingdom" then was one who did not seek children, and this means the one who abstained from sexual intercourse.[35]

Matthew did not expect all church members to follow the pronouncement in 19:12, as the line "Let anyone accept this who can" indicates. I do not think, however, the line is authentic: the rest of the Jesus tradition does not appear to make radical demands conditional: do it if you can, but if you can't, don't worry.

Similarly, the Gospels do not privilege childbearing. According to Luke 11:27–28 (NRSV), "A woman in the crowd raised her voice and said to him [Jesus], 'Blessed is the womb that bore you and the breasts that nursed you!' But he said, 'Blessed rather are those who hear the word of God and obey it!'" This statement, also cited in *Gospel of Thomas* 79 (where Luke 23:29 is added), recollects Jesus' ideal of the new family.[36] The major point of the saying is, probably, that honor and blessing should not be based on family lines; for women as well, one's ethic rather than one's fertility is to be valued. But the saying is also consistent with a negative view of procreation. In an apocalyptic context, Jesus correspondingly blesses the wombs that never gave birth and the breasts that never nursed (Luke 23:29). Unlike his prophetic predecessors, the one miracle Jesus does *not* do is cure infertility.

Jesus' sexual asceticism may be seen as part of a tradent

in early Christianity and Judaism: much of 1 Corinthians,[37] Revelation's 144,000 male virgins (14:4), and Philip's virgin daughters (Acts 21:9) all indicate a preference for celibacy.[38] Although the Dead Sea Scrolls themselves do not prohibit intercourse, Josephus, Philo, and Pliny agree that the Essenes were celibate.[39] Sexual asceticism is likewise consistent with Jesus' interest in a new Eden. While Rabbinic sources read Genesis as indicating that Adam and Eve had sexual relations in the Garden, earlier Jewish texts do not (2 *Bar* 56:6; *Jub* 3; perhaps 4Q265).[40]

As with the question of divorce, Jesus' preference for celibacy is, finally, less the issue. The major question is its rationale. Intimately familiar with the Hebrew Scriptures, Jesus may have considered himself a new Moses or (less likely) a true priest seeking a true Temple. In either case, he might endorse celibacy. Before Mt. Sinai, the people of Israel were told to refrain from intercourse (in gendered terms, "Do not touch a woman"; cf. Exod 19:15), and priests needed to keep themselves apart from sexual intercourse before performing specific Temple duties. However, his various comments on human sexuality (celibacy, divorce, separation of families, childbirth, etc.) do not all match these models.

As a resident of the Hellenized Mediterranean world, Jesus may have subscribed to the prevailing medical views that semen production is at best a necessary evil and that intercourse occasions for both men and women weakness and loss of spiritual vigor.[41] Yet the "professional" medical opinion may not have been shared by popular culture, and there is no evidence Jesus even knew of such ideas.

Likely among Jesus' followers were fellow Galileans whose familial structures had been disrupted by the increasing pressures of urbanization and colonialism. In this context, abstinence is practical: given disintegration of family ties and land ownership, children are an economic burden. Then again, disruption of peasant life or even familial separation under economic pressure does not necessarily create an ascetic impulse. The contrary effect is equally plausible if not more likely. Apart from millenarian implications, the problems of colonialism do not typically translate into calls for asceticism. We therefore return to our thesis that Jesus be seen as an apocalyptic, eschatological prophet. In this worldview, asceticism would be expected.

Jesus commended celibacy. What then should the third caller do? He might, for example, follow the Church and the canon and not just statements in the Gospels taken out of context. Although celibacy remained a major impulse in Church development, those who compiled the canon decided to include the Pastoral Epistles but not the Apocryphal Acts: childbirth, and therefore sexual intercourse, became not only encouraged but necessary for salvation (1 Timothy 2). Also to the caller's relief, I noted that celibacy is, even in Matthew 19's saying on eunuchs, a spiritual gift. Finally, I advised him to see both a pastoral-care specialist and a caterer.

Likely I will soon get a call citing Genesis 1:28 and asking about birth control.

Reception

Jesus gathered a small but loyal following of fellow Jews who sought to incarnate the *basileia*, the kingdom of heaven, on earth. They preached a joyous attitude toward life, community support and solidarity and a view of others based on actions, not on pronouncements, birth, or wealth. With this message and this lifestyle, women took their place among Jesus' followers. His association with women, in and of itself, is unremarkable.

But the times were dangerous for popular prophets and their followers, as the preemptive strike Herod Antipas took against John the Baptist testifies. In such times and for such people, marriage is a luxury, and children are a liability. But Jesus' sexual ethic stems from more than political challenge: he anticipated major change through divine intervention into history. Marriage would soon pass away as we all become angels in heaven.

For those Christians who want the Word to become flesh in the twentieth century, it seems to me that the turn toward the celebration of marriage and childbirth for those lacking the spiritual gift of celibacy, a more open view of divorce especially in cases of domestic abuse, and the increasing role of women in the Church would not be inconsistent with the scriptural model beginning with Genesis. Would the historical Jesus agree? I would like to think so, given his willingness to make unpopular pronouncements, his concerns for justice, and his prophetic critique of exploitation and of self-righteous religious leadership. Then again, this may be my wish, not his view.

For those who seek to enact the more radical statements, such as those on divorce, into law, historical inquiry provides some context at least for those willing to consider it. If we do not live in the same culture, and with the same worldview, as Jesus and his earliest followers, then we must, necessarily, adapt. This has always been the role of the Church. And for those who are not interested in history, in interpretation, in human needs, for those who insist on their own literalistic interpretation of *select* passages in the canon, then before they spout a historical anti-Jewish apologetic, condemn those seeking exit from abusive relationships, and forbid committed partners from sanctifying their relationships, my advice remains, "Sell all you have and give to the poor; leave your parents, children, and spouse; pluck out your eye and cut off your hand; be perfect, and then come back and make your case."

Notes

1. A Rabbinic expression equivalent to the *a fortiori* argument "how much more."

2. Http://divinity.lib.vanderbilt.edu/Carpenter/index.htm.

3. Tikva Frymer-Kensky, "Sex and Sexuality," *Anchor Bible Dictionary* (New York: Doubleday, 1992) 5:1144–46.

4. J. Cheryl Exum, *Fragmented Women: Feminist (Sub)versions of Biblical Narratives* (Sheffield: JSOT Press, 1993).

5. The opening of such questions as academically viable topics is due in great measure to Elisabeth Schüssler Fiorenza, *In Memory of Her: A Feminist Theological Reconstruction of Christian Origins* (New York: Crossroad, 1984); *Jesus: Miriam's Child, Sophia's Prophet: Critical Issues in Feminist Christology* (New York: Continuum, 1994).

6. Remnants of this view appear in much of the work of Marcus

Borg, which has served to awaken in many Christians new interest in and respect for the Jesus tradition. Ben Witherington III, with whom I frequently disagree, here cogently recognizes that Borg's Jesus, "in his advocacy of compassion, was opposed to purity systems of all sorts." Witherington then demonstrates why Borg's view is untenable. See Witherington, *The Jesus Quest: The Third Search for the Historical Jesus,* 2d ed. (Downers Grove, Ill.: InterVarsity Press, 1997) 104.

7. Judith Plaskow, "Blaming the Jews for the Birth of Patriarchy," *Lilith* 7 (1980) 11–12, 14–17; "Anti-Judaism in Feminist Christian Interpretation," in *Searching the Scriptures,* vol. 1, *A Feminist Introduction,* ed. E. Schüssler Fiorenza (New York: Crossroad, 1993) 117–29; Susannah Heschel, "Anti-Judaism in Christian Feminist Theology," *Tikkun* 5.3 (1990) 25–28, 95–97; Amy-Jill Levine, "Yeast of Eden: Jesus, Second Temple Judaism, and Women," *Biblical Interpretation* 2 (1994) 8–33; "Lilies of the Field and Wandering Jews: Biblical Scholarship, Women's Roles, and Social Location," in *Transformative Encounters: Jesus and Women Re-viewed,* ed. I. R. Kitzberger (Leiden: Brill, 1999) 329–52.

8. E. P. Sanders, *Paul and Palestinian Judaism: A Comparison of Patterns of Religion* (Philadelphia: Fortress, 1977).

9. N. T. Wright, *Jesus and the Victory of God,* Christian Origins and the Question of God 2 (Minneapolis: Fortress, 1996) 52, following Bruce Malina and Jerome Neyrey, in *The Social World of Luke-Acts: Models for Interpretation,* ed. Jerome Neyrey (Peabody, Mass.: Hendrickson, 1991).

10. Cf. John 11:1–12:8. See the helpful descriptions by Carolyn Osiek and David L. Balch, *Families in the New Testament World: Households and House Churches,* The Family, Religion and Culture Series (Louisville: Westminster/John Knox, 1997) 6–11.

11. Cf. E. P. Sanders, *Jewish Law from Jesus to the Mishnah: Five Studies* (London: SCM; Philadelphia: Trinity Press International, 1990); *Judaism: Practice and Belief 63 B.C.E.–70 C.E.* (London: SCM; Philadelphia: Trinity Press International, 1992).

12. Cf. James H. Charlesworth, ed., *Jesus' Jewishness: Exploring the Place of Jesus within Early Judaism* (Philadelphia: American Interfaith Institute; New York: Crossroad, 1991); *Jesus within Judaism: New Light from Exciting Archaeological Discoveries,* Anchor Bible Reference Library (Garden City, N.Y.: Doubleday, 1988).

13. John Dominic Crossan, *The Historical Jesus: The Life of a Mediterranean Jewish Peasant* (San Francisco: HarperSanFrancisco, 1991).

14. Amy-Jill Levine, "Discharging Responsibility: Matthean Jesus, Biblical Law, and Hemorrhaging Woman," in *Treasures New and Old: Contributions to Matthean Studies,* ed. D. R. Bauer and M. A. Powell, SBL Symposium Series (Atlanta: Scholars, 1996) 379–97.

15. See Levine, "Yeast of Eden," 8–33.

16. Crossan, *Historical Jesus,* 298. Wright, following an unpublished paper by Jerome Neyrey, condemns Crossan for "celebrating sexual ambiguity or homosexuality" in relation to the historical Jesus (*Jesus and the Victory,* 54); this is not Crossan's point. His *Historical Jesus* discusses Secret Mark but divorces the historical Jesus from the erotic overcoat worn by the naked young man in the garden (330ff.).

17. Some commentators claim that Mark's note that women cannot divorce their husbands must be an addition to Jesus' original words (now found in Matthew and Luke or, for some, Q) because Jewish women in the Second Temple period did not have this right. But this claim has been demonstrated false for Diaspora settings, and quite likely within the wider Mediterranean culture that also engulfed Judea, some women there too sought divorce (perhaps from Roman courts).

18. Jesus' association with prostitutes remains debated among historians. Matt 21:31 associates John the Baptist with "tax collectors and prostitutes," but the phrase may be an expression of inclusivity for male and female sinners. It is not clear that the woman "of the city" who anoints Jesus (Luke 7:36–50) is a prostitute.

19. See Marcus Borg, *Meeting Jesus Again for the First Time: The Historical Jesus and the Heart of Contemporary Faith* (San Francisco: HarperSanFrancisco, 1994) 57. Cf. Crossan, *Historical Jesus,* 301–2, incorrectly, on Jewish women's inability to obtain a divorce and, following John Kloppenborg, on the attack on "androcentric honour whose debilitating effects went far beyond the situation of divorce." On Jewish women obtaining divorce (e.g., Salome, the sister of Herod the Great: Herodias, daughter of Agrippa I, and perhaps Shelamzion of Nahal Hever fame), see John J. Collins, "Marriage, Divorce, and Family in Second Temple Judaism," in *Families in Ancient Israel,* ed. L. G. Perdue and others, The Family, Religion, and Culture Series (Louisville: Westminster/John Knox, 1997) 120.

20. Detailed discussion in Collins, "Marriage, Divorce," 117–20. The pronouncements appear in the context of a debate between the Houses of Hillel and Shammai (see *M. Git* 9–10).

21. Divorce may have increased under the pressures of the Bar Cochba Revolt of the early second century C.E. On divorce documents, see Collins, "Marriage, Divorce," 111.

22. Ibid., 107–12, 115–19.

23. Ibid., 112.

24. This notice is similar to his citation of Mic 7:5–6 on disruption between parents and children (cf. Matt 10:34–39; Luke 12:51–53; 14:25–27; and cf. *Gospel of Thomas* 55, 101).

25. Most commentators assume Luke added "wife," although separation of spouses in the context of millenarian piety is hardly un-

usual. On the replacement of traditional families with fictive kin by millenarian groups and sectarian movements generally, see Dale C. Allison Jr., *Jesus of Nazareth: Millenarian Prophet* (Minneapolis: Fortress, 1998); and sources cited there. This volume, just published, is the first sustained study of Jesus and asceticism.

26. Wright connects the injunction with Jesus' vision of the "new heart" and the inauguration of the "new covenant" (*Jesus and the Victory*, 285–87). Wright also suggests that the teaching was cryptic, given the political liability of arguing against divorce with Antipas's rule (*Jesus and the Victory*, 397–98; cf. Mark 6:18, 21–29).

27. Osiek and Balch, *Families*, 124.

28. Witherington, *Jesus Quest*, 59.

29. Materials cited in support of marriage, such as John 2, are not decisive. The historicity of the singularly attested account is debatable, and attendance at a wedding is no more an endorsement of the marriage than eating at the home of a tax collector or sinner is an endorsement of tax collecting or sin.

30. The clause may have addressed (gentile) marriages rendered illegal by Levitical consanguinity legislation. It may also reflect Augustan law making adultery a crime, such that the man who did not divorce and prosecute his adulterous wife could be accused of pimping.

31. For texts and discussion, see W. D. Davies and Dale. C. Allison Jr., *A Critical and Exegetical Commentary on the Gospel according to Saint Matthew*, New International Critical Commentary Series 1 (Edinburgh: T. & T. Clark, 1988) 524.

32. See Hans Dieter Betz's denial that the idiom lies behind the verse in question; *The Sermon on the Mount*, Hermeneia Series (Minneapolis: Fortress, 1995) 238 n. 335.

33. See Josephus *War* 3.374, on the "chaste bodies" of the world-to-come. Witherington sees the comparison as indicating not "asexuality or lack of married condition" but "immortality" (*Jesus Quest*, 169). His appeal to Philo is inconsequential, his emphasis is not supported by other textual materials, and his view erases the specifics of the comparison itself. Also unconvincing are those arguments that see Jesus as looking forward to the end of "patriarchal" marriage in which women are objectified as tokens of exchange; this may be the result of the statement, but less clear is its function as motivation.

34. Crossan, *Historical Jesus*, 267, in discussion of *Thomas*; the comments here extend Crossan's point back to the historical Jesus.

35. There is no indication that birth control is intended.

36. Crossan, *Historical Jesus*, 299–300.

37. Paul's notice that other apostles take a "sister-wife" (*adelphēn gynaika*, 1 Cor 9:5), although not often cited as an example of celibacy, is likely to be precisely this.

38. Matters would also be clearer if we knew which, if any, of the noncanonical gospels contain comments from Jesus' lips. For example, in the *Gospel of Thomas*, Jesus suggests that Mary Magdalene must become "male" (give up her female identity, probably through radical asceticism, and thereby become an androgyne, like *ha-adam*, "the earthling" in Eden, prior to the separation into male and female bodies) to enter the kingdom. Even for those who see *Thomas* as reflecting historical material, this verse is usually seen as part of a later redactor's interests (e.g., it is consistent with other concerns about celibacy and asceticism in *Thomas*; then again, this is hardly a definitive reason for elimination).

39. Sources and discussion in Collins, "Marriage, Divorce," 128–35.

40. See discussion and notes in ibid., 128–29; G. Anderson, "Celibacy or Consummation in the Garden? Reflections on Early Jewish and Christian Interpretations of the Garden of Eden," *Harvard Theological Review* 82 (1989) 121–48.

41. See Osiek and Balch, *Families*, 104–7. The ancient medical view has, ironically, been preserved primarily by athletes.

Chapter 4

The Historical Jesus:
Sources and a Sketch

James H. Charlesworth

Introduction

Scholars have clarified the parameters of Jesus' life. You may ask, "Where did he live?" We have the answer: he lived in ancient Palestine. You may continue your questioning, "When did he live?" We again know the answer: from near the end of King Herod's reign in ca. 4 B.C.E. to sometime during the prefecture of Pontius Pilate (26–36 C.E.). It is also clear, according to our extant sources, that Jesus wrote no book, no treatise, and not one letter. These solid — and internationally recognized — conclusions are merely the basics from over two hundred years of independent study that is free from the dictates of the Church and dogmatism.

While some results of research are encouraging, others are disappointing. In fact, some research has resulted in painful and disappointing conclusions. For example, it is now internationally recognized that Jesus' disciples did not write the Gospels that later generations attributed to them.[1] Even today, many

Christians resist the truth that the apostle Matthew did not write the First Gospel and that the apostle John did not compose the Fourth Gospel.[2] Their resistance is due, in part, to the pain such realization often causes them. And most of us would have been pleased if historical research had added credence to the idea that the Gospels of Matthew and John obtained their name because the apostles actually composed them.[3]

We are now led to a focused question: How do we discover reliable traditions about Jesus? These traditions are almost always preserved in the Gospels that postdate Jesus by at least thirty years. It is true that the disciples were interested in proclaiming Jesus of Nazareth the Christ — that is, the Messiah expected according to some Jewish texts. This attractive fact for Christians precludes the possibility that the Evangelists were interested in writing a biography of Jesus. Most Christians, I imagine, would rather have meaningful interpretations of Jesus that help them grasp their own faith commitment than a historical biography of Jesus. Hence, the disappointment at having to give up on a biography of Jesus written by a disciple develops into an appreciation of the faith commitments of Jesus' followers. These reflections should not suggest that only we moderns have an advanced sense of historiography. The early Jews, including those who followed Jesus' teachings, knew about the problems with creative histories and with distortions of history. Josephus, at least, and Luke, probably, knew Polybius's work on historiography and the sophisticated historiography he developed in Book XII.[4]

Our task then is to sift the Gospels in search of sayings and actions of Jesus that with some probability derive ultimately from him, with some alteration, of course, by the Evangelists. Our goal is not to discern the precise words he used. The ill-conceived search for *ipsissima verba Jesu* — that is, Jesus' own unaltered words — ignores the continuum of probability that the historian and New Testament expert employs.[5] Our purpose today is to seek the intentionality in Jesus' authentic words and actions. Contemporary scholars thus tend to ask, "What did Jesus intend to communicate to whom by a certain saying or an action?" After all, most of us are not so much interested in the precise words Jesus chose to use as in what he tried to communicate to his contemporaries.

Today there is a consensus among the leading experts in "Jesus research," the technical term I gave to the new phase of studying Jesus in his context.[6] The consensus is that we do have considerable historical knowledge about Jesus, and this knowledge is neither irrelevant nor odd within the world of first-century Judaism. This consensus I tried to assess in an earlier Faith and Scholarship Colloquy published under the title *Images of Jesus Today*.[7] E. P. Sanders assessed the consensus succinctly. I believe his assessment is accurate: "The dominant view today seems to be that we can know pretty well what Jesus was out to accomplish, that we can know a lot about what he said, and that those two things make sense within the world of first-century Judaism."[8]

Nomenclature

When commencing our examination of Jesus, we should clarify our major terms. "The Jesus of history" means the Jesus who lived in ancient Palestine before 70 C.E. The only way we could confront that person would be to change ourselves completely into first-century Jews and to be transported back to Galilee in the twenties in order to meet Jesus. That is and always will be impossible. Even if someday we might be able to accomplish time travel, we will always be from another time and place than Jesus. "The historical Jesus" is the Jesus constructed, with acumen and after lengthy research, by specialists on the New Testament. This figure will always be different from the Jesus of history who lived back then and over there. "The Christ of faith" denotes the Jesus who confronts us in faith and the one we meet in the preached word.

The New Testament expert also knows that no clear or absolute distinction can ever be made between the historical Jesus and the Christ of faith, despite the attempts of Martin Kähler and some claims made by Rudolf Bultmann and his students. I am impressed that virtually all confessions tend to have a mixture of history and faith; for example, on Sunday morning many Christians rise and confess that Jesus was crucified under Pontius Pilate and was raised on the third day. The first confession belongs to the category of history. The second is a confession of faith.

Scholars have indicated that the historical Jesus is a Jewish male who instilled faith in the Jewish God and called fellow Jews to a deeper covenantal relationship with their creating God. What I am appealing to now is more precision in our use of language. I am well aware that not only in the popular mind but also in erudite tomes the "historical Jesus" and the "Jesus of history" are confusedly used as synonymous expressions.

For more precision two additional terms may be introduced. "The sayings of Jesus" is the term to denote the words of Jesus preserved in our sources and all the sayings attributed to him. "Jesus' sayings," in contrast, denote those sayings of Jesus that warrant being recognized as originating ultimately with Jesus. Recently, many scholars are persuaded that there were some controls for transmitting Jesus' sayings so that we do have reliable information regarding what he taught.[9] It is no longer wise to attribute the creation of sayings of Jesus to the early Christian prophets, as did Bultmann sometimes and his followers frequently. David Hill and David E. Aune, who have published detailed research on the early Christian prophets, report that careful research reveals that early "Christian" prophets are not those who created Jesus sayings.[10] Thus, the theory that oracles of "Christian" prophets uttered in the name of Jesus were "mingled with the sayings of Jesus" is exposed to be "largely the creative imagination of scholars."[11]

Sources

What are the sources from which we might sift traditions in search of the historical Jesus? Where can we find early and basically reliable information about Jesus?

First, the four gospels in the New Testament are not our only sources, but they are our fundamental primary sources and always take precedence over all other sources. Outdated is the contention that the Fourth Gospel contains no historical accuracy.[12] The Gospels are now available in the *Novum Testamentum Graece* (*The Greek New Testament*), in Swanson's *New Testament Greek Manuscripts,* and in the New Revised Standard Version (NRSV) and other modern translations.[13]

Second, the writings of Josephus, the first-century Jew and historian, are clearly our most important source for the study of social phenomena in the first century, especially up to and including the First Jewish War against Rome from 66 to 70, or 74 C.E. when Masada fell. His books are complex; they should neither be taken at face value nor dismissed as mere Jewish propaganda for the Greek or Roman reader.[14] His topographical descriptions, especially of Gamla, are often amazingly accurate, but his description of Jewish thought as philosophies divided into four groups is misleading. Josephus's writings are easily available in William Whiston's *The Works of Josephus* and in Greek with English in the Loeb Classical Library.[15] Josephus did refer to Jesus, but his account was edited by scribes who painstakingly copied his account of Jesus. Thus I have concluded that the *Testimonium Flavianum* as extant betrays Christian editing, but it primarily preserves Josephus's reference to Jesus.[16]

Third, the documents in the New Testament Apocrypha and Pseudepigrapha embellish and expand the New Testament accounts, but there are some extracanonical sayings of Jesus (*agrapha*) that derive from Jesus and have not been altered any more than the sayings of Jesus recorded in the intracanonical gospels.[17] Along with numerous scholars, namely John Dominic Crossan and Helmut Koester,[18] I have tried to illustrate this point, especially in my *Jesus within Judaism*[19] and in "Jesus in the Agrapha and Apocryphal Gospels."[20] The only apocryphal gospel that seems, in my view, to preserve authentic Jesus sayings is the *Gospel of Thomas*. This gospel was discovered in Greek about a century ago (Oxyrhynchus Papyri 1, 654, and 655) and then in Coptic about fifty years ago (Nag Hammadi Codex 2, second tractate).[21] Unfortunately, excessive claims have been made about the authenticity of the Apocrypha by some scholars.

This penchant for exaggeration is unfortunate since other scholars could point it out and then retreat from an examination of the apocryphal traditions to defend the canon as the only primary source for Jesus research. The result is the tendency by too many experts to focus myopically only on the canonical gospels.

Where can one find the New Testament apocryphal writings?[22] These are now conveniently available in collections edited recently by Wilhelm Schneemelcher and translated from the German by R. McL. Wilson.[23] M. R. James's valuable collection of New Testament apocryphal works has been reedited by J. K. Elliott.[24] And Helmut Koester has published a selection of apocryphal gospels.[25]

Fourth, the Mishnah is another collection of Jewish writings that are important for ascertaining life under the Torah and in and around Jerusalem when the temple was still standing.[26] This collection of Jewish writings was completed shortly after 200 C.E., but it often preserves reliable earlier traditions. Today we have the classic translation of the Mishnah by Herbert Danby and a more literal translation of it by Jacob Neusner.[27] These four distinct collections of writings all postdate Jesus and always by decades. At least two sources may date from the period of the 30s to the 50s, and that would be within about a decade of Jesus' life. The first is a source preserved only in Matthew and Luke. It is a source we call "Q," perhaps because it is a "source" (which in German is *Quelle*) of sayings of Jesus not found in Mark but shared by Matthew and Luke.[28] The other early source is the "Signs Source," which is preserved only in the Gospel of John.[29] This source seems to be a separate work inherited by the author John; it numbers Jesus' miracles, refers to them as signs, and the numbers given to the signs in John do not neatly fit the account of Jesus' miracles enumerated in it.

There are tracts and testimonies that circulated as early as the 30s in Palestine, usually only or originally in oral forms. Some were collections of Jesus' parables; others were collections of his miracles. Many of these tracts can be discerned in Mark because of the clustering of parables and miracle stories within it.

To perceive what Jesus was like, the scholar cannot work only with documents that postdate 70 C.E., which is a crucial time in history. Not only was the First Gospel written about then, but in 70 Jerusalem and the temple were burned.[30] Thereafter Judaism was changed markedly. What are the documents that derive from Jesus' time and help us understand what Judaism was like when he was teaching in lower Galilee?

First, we have thirteen Old Testament apocryphal writings that have been preserved in copies of the Septuagint. These are reliably transmitted by Christian scribes, but the Jewish documents in this category antedate Jesus by sometimes as much as a century. Editions of the Old Testament Apocrypha have been published by the RSV and the NRSV through HarperCollins and Oxford.[31]

Second, the Old Testament Pseudepigrapha are sixty-five documents that were composed by Jews and sometimes edited and expanded by Christians. They date from ca. 250 B.C.E. to centuries after the documents collected into the New Testament were composed. While once disparaged as only fringe Jewish writings, the Pseudepigrapha are now perceived to represent the thoughts of many Jews, some living in Palestine and some in the Diaspora. It is clear that the study of the Jewish Pseudepigrapha is essential for comprehending Jesus and his time.[32] We know the antiquity of some of the books because Aramaic and Hebrew copies have been found in the eleven caves that preserved for almost two thousand years the Dead Sea Scrolls. However, usually we must work on Christian copies of these ancient Jewish writings from the time of Jesus. This is unfortunate since frequently scribes have altered or added to the original Jewish work. This editing is obvious in the *Testaments of Twelve Patriarchs*. The most complete collection of these writings was edited by myself and published by Doubleday under the title *The Old Testament Pseudepigrapha*.[33]

Are there no documents that date from Jesus' time and are still in the form that the ancient Jews knew? Yes! That is why the Dead Sea Scrolls are so significant for Jesus research. These Jewish documents are precisely the same ones held by Jesus' contemporaries. We now have about six hundred documents from the time of Jesus, and they were often considered inspired and full of God's word for his people.

Even though Jesus and his disciples are never mentioned in the Dead Sea Scrolls, these writings are invaluable for Jesus research. They reveal in astounding ways the conceptions and perceptions of Jesus' contemporary Jews. They also reveal the dreams and aspirations of his fellow Jews. It is from these documents, supplemented by insights garnered from the Apocrypha and Pseudepigrapha, that we can comprehend Jesus' eschatology and apocalypsology,[34] that is, Jesus' view of reality, the future, and his proclamation that God's rule or kingdom is breaking now into the present.[35] Jesus shared with his fellow Jews the perspective that only God can and will announce who is the Messiah and when the endtime will commence. Thus, the Jewish literature from Jesus' time, especially the Dead Sea Scrolls, is the most valuable source for helping us reconstruct the world in which Jesus lived and taught.[36]

The critical edition of the texts and translations of the Dead Sea Scrolls is being published under the auspices of the Princeton Theological Seminary, thanks to a distinguished group of internationally renowned Dead Sea Scrolls experts. Edited by myself, the critical work is being published by Mohr (Siebeck) and Westminster/John Knox.[37] One-volume, English only, collections of the scrolls have been published by Michael Wise, Martin G. Abegg, and Edward M. Cook through HarperCollins, by Florentino García Martínez through Brill, and Geza Vermes through the Penguin Press. Vermes' *The Complete Dead Sea Scrolls in English,* which appeared in 1997, is in many ways the best of these collections.[38]

Another source for studying Jesus is often overlooked. It is the Greek Magical Papyri. These documents postdate Jesus but supply a valuable insight into the fears and superstitions of those living near the time of Jesus. These papyri are characterized by the belief that magic is necessary to live safe and successful lives. Usually the author reveals how one can control demons, devils, and evil spirits through magical incantations and esoteric sounds. The magical incantation can also cure illnesses or obtain other desirable results. Such beliefs are intermittently mirrored in the New Testament Gospels and in Josephus's writings. They spring forth in several Jewish apocryphal works, such as the *Testament of Solomon*. If Jesus did not think he was a magician, as Morton Smith claimed,[39] it is nevertheless clear that some of his contemporaries most likely assumed he was a magician, associated him with magic,[40] or perceived him as one like Solomon.[41] A convenient selection in English translation of some of these Greek magical documents is published by Hans Dieter Betz.[42]

Finally, there is another source that is essential in understanding and portraying the intellectual world of Jesus' time. It is archaeology.[43] Some interest in archaeology usually is brought with visitors and pilgrims to Jerusalem, and if not, the massive four-hundred-year-old walls will awaken in most a sense of ancient history and archaeology.[44] Since the late 1960s excavators in Galilee,[45] Samaria,[46] and Judea[47] have made discoveries that have revolutionized our understanding of first-century life in Palestine before the horrible events of 70 C.E. that brought an end to Jesus' Judaism. The archaeological discoveries are reported and assessed in two recent major multivolume publications: *The Oxford Encyclopedia of Archaeology in the Near East* and, the more helpful work for biblical experts, *The New Encyclopedia of Archaeological Excavations in the Holy Land*. A handy and authoritative summary, focused on Jesus research, is John J. Rousseau and Rami Arav's *Jesus and His World: An Archaeological and Cultural Dictionary*.[48]

A succinct review of the importance of archaeology for perceiving Jesus in his time may be organized into realia. That is, a convenient and objective means of assessing the importance of archaeological discoveries for Jesus research is to focus on the objects unearthed in ancient Palestine that help us understand the social and religious life of Jesus' contemporaries. It is obvious that among the methods the historian must use in understanding Jesus in his time are the insights learned from sociologists and anthropologists.[49] Another means to assess the importance of archaeology in Jesus research is to focus on what we know archaeologically about the cities and villages in which he lived and worked.

Excavations in the so-called Holy Land help us immeasurably to imagine and then reconstruct the life of people living in Palestine before 70 C.E. We can hold and study the utensils of average daily life, such as clay pots, cups, and knives for eating. We can imagine and picture the way women looked because of the recovery of braided hair, leather sandals with iron nails, and woven garments with colored ornamentations. We can envision them beautifying their face and body because of the recovery of mirrors, gold earrings, bracelets, necklaces, and cosmetic bottles with iron applicators.[50] We may even experience the approximate scent of their perfume, thanks to the study of perfume remains found in a clay vessel recovered near Qumran, which were chemically analyzed, recreated, and distributed under the name of *Abishag*.[51]

We can ponder the busy marketplace as we hold the money that Jesus' contemporaries used in transactions: especially the many silver and gold coins bearing the portrait of Roman emperors, like Nero and Vespasian, and other bronze coins with Jewish symbols. Holding these coins we can relive Jesus' question about whose image is on the coin. When the reply was "Caesar," we hear again Jesus' command to give to Caesar what is Caesar's and to God what is God's. Thousands of such coins have been catalogued, studied, and explained in numerous volumes, most notably those written by Yaakou Meshorer.[52]

We can reflect on the struggle to obtain and conserve water in arid and semiarid countries, as we examine the small and large aqueducts and also the immense cisterns for holding water. Some of these were built by the Romans or their quislings like Pontius Pilate and some by religious Jews. We have a much better grasp of fishing on the Sea of Galilee, thanks to the recovery of a boat. It is a wooden fishing boat built in the first century B.C.E. and used by Jewish fishermen in the Sea of Galilee not far from where Jesus lived in Capernaum and precisely where one of his closest admirers once lived, namely, Mary Magdalene. It is rather shallow, making it possible to cast large fishing nets but precarious when any storm might arise on the lake.[53] Thus we are brought much closer to such stories as the disciples panicking because their boat was about to sink (Mark 4:35–41).

Archaeologists often have a somber tale to relate. The horrors of life in or near Jesus' time are often all too real. We come face-to-face with human skulls, human bones, iron spears, arrow heads, ballistic missiles, charred timbers, and frescoed walls now black from the heat and conflagration of an inferno. Life under the occupation of Rome — especially after the First Jewish Revolt of 66 C.E. — may be rightly compared to hell. We come much closer to perceiving what Jesus meant when he said that the one who lives by the sword will die by the sword (Matt 26:52).

Let us now turn to the question, How has archaeological work in the Levant on ancient cities and villages helped us better comprehend Jesus in his time? Archaeological excavations in Caesarea Maritima,[54] Capernaum,[55] Sepphoris,[56] Nazareth,[57] Scythopolis, Sebaste, Herodian Jericho, the Herodium,[58] Masada,[59] and especially in the Old City of Jerusalem reveal,[60] often in astounding ways, the life of people living in Palestine before 70. Sometimes I am amazed by the massive building projects begun and completed by Herod the Great. The temple, for example, was described by Josephus in terms that former professors dismissed as enthusiastic hyperbole. But now we know how massive and impressive that structure was. A stone has been found in Herod's western retaining wall, just to the north of the Wailing Wall, which has been estimated to weigh between four hundred and six hundred tons. That is astounding since the heaviest stone in the Pyramids weighs about fifty tons, at the most. Again, we pause to imagine what Jesus and his Galilean fishermen saw and marveled at in Jerusalem: "Look, Teacher, what massive stones and what massive buildings" (Mark 13:1, my translation).[61]

Archaeology helps us rethink Jesus' trial. Excavators have found Caiaphus's ossuary in which his bones were most likely recovered. We also possess a stone with a first-century inscription that preserves Pilate's name and office (*praefectus*). We can conclude with relative certainty that Jesus was crucified on the stone revered in the Church of the Holy Sepulcher. Why is that conclusion possible and even probable? It is because of the discovery of a wall that enclosed within Jerusalem the area covered by the Church of the Holy Sepulcher, and the wall dates a little over a decade *after* Jesus' crucifixion. That means that traditional Golgotha in 30 C.E. was outside of the walls of Jerusalem. The conclusion that the traditional Golgotha is reliable also is enhanced by the examination of a quarry beneath the stone on which tradition indicates Jesus was crucified. Thus this ancient tradition that situates Jesus' crucifixion on the stone housed now by the Church of the Holy Sepulcher did not originate ex nihilo in the fourth century C.E., when the church was constructed under the guidance of Helena, the mother of the Emperor Constantine.

Archaeological excavators have revealed the average life of Jews and others during Jesus' time. We can see and even walk on streets that were used in the first century but have lain buried for almost two millennia. The thin walls of houses in Capernaum that now can be seen after nearly two millennia would not support tile roofs, as would the walls in Sepphoris and Jerusalem; thus, they would demand thatched roofs. We can now more accurately assess episodes placed by the Evangelists in Capernaum. For example, recall the famous story of the efforts of the friends of a lame man who were able to dig through a roof to see Jesus with his disciples. They were thus able to lower their friend to Jesus for healing (Mark 2:1–12).

Other archaeological discoveries help us fill in the religious regulations found emphasized in the Jewish apocryphal works, in the Dead Sea Scrolls, and especially in the Mishnah. From the eleven Qumran caves archaeologists have retrieved phylacteries in their clay boxes, reminding us of the literalistic interpretation of the Torah. Jews literally bound the Law on their foreheads (cf. Exod 13:9, 16; Deut 6:8; 11:18). The recovery of expensive glass and stone vessels reminds us that only these impermeable containers protect their contents from pollution and danger. As we look at the massive stone vessels unearthed in the Upper City of Jerusalem and at Qumran, we are reminded of the warning in the *Temple Scroll* that all items in earthen vessels are worthless if an impure woman enters a home. The text is riveting in its sociological implications; that is, pious Jews would need to check on the state of purity of a house before entering it. Here is the passage in the *Temple Scroll:*

> And if a woman is pregnant, and her child dies in her womb, all the days on which it is dead, she is unclean like a grave; and every house she comes into is unclean, with all its furnishings, for seven days. And anyone who touches it shall be unclean until the evening; and if he enters the house with her, he shall be unclean seven days.... And to all the furnishings, clothing and (objects of) skin and all work of goat('s hair) you shall do according to the ordinance of this law. And all earthen vessels shall be broken, for they are unclean and cannot become clean again for ever. (11QTemple 50.10–18)[62]

Other religious regulations that are mentioned in our literary sources are now observable, even palpable, in the light of archaeological research. Most importantly, *mikvaot*, ritual baths for purification, have been found in many places, notably at Masada, Herodian Jericho, Qumran, and especially in Old Jerusalem. These *mikvaot* date from the Herodian period and prove the increasing legislation and mores for purity in Jesus' time. The synagogue built of basalt stones in Gamla and of ashlar blocks or cut stones in the Herodium and Masada prove archaeologically that synagogues were built as religious buildings in Jesus' time and that Jews did not simply gather in houses.[63] The base of the synagogue in Capernaum in which Jesus probably taught now appears in horizontal basalt black stones beneath a later white-stoned majestic basilical building that was clearly a synagogue.

Excavators have brought home, sometimes too poignantly, the horrors of first-century Jewish life before 70. Gamla and Masada stand abandoned and lifeless. They are like silent sentinels of the suicides committed there in 67 and 74, respectively. Excavations in Jerusalem, especially the temple area and the Upper City, uncovered burned timbers and the awful conflagration of the first-century holocaust. The archaeologists who excavated the Burnt House in Upper Jerusalem were moved by the smell of burning timbers that had lain hidden since the late summer of 70 C.E. The bone from a woman's arm was found near a doorway.

The importance of archaeological excavations for Jesus research is obvious, and my published comments can be found primarily in two books: *Jesus within Judaism: New Light from Exciting Archaeological Discoveries* and in *Jesus and the Dead Sea Scrolls*. I am convinced that the archaeological discoveries significantly help us understand the trustworthiness of some of the Jesus traditions. For example, in 30 C.E. Philip, Herod's son, renamed Bethsaida in honor of the wife of Caesar Augustus, Livia/Julia.[64] During the reign of Herod the Great she had sent from Rome some of her most valuable furniture to Herod to be placed in Sebaste.[65] After 30 C.E., Bethsaida was known as Julia. Its status also changed from a mere village (*kōmē*) to a city (*polis*). Josephus often calls the city both Bethsaida and Julia, but the Evangelists always refer to it only as Bethsaida. In fact, the name Julia for this city never appears in the New Testament. It is also informative to note that Mark, perhaps the earliest Gospel, calls Bethsaida a "village," but later Gospels, Luke and John, call it a "city" (Mark 8:23; Luke 9:10; John 1:44).

The Evangelists report that numerous disciples came from Bethsaida, namely Philip, Andrew, and Simon Peter (John 1:44). Because they were partners with Andrew and Simon Peter, James and John the sons of Zebedee may also be from Bethsaida. Is the fact that the Evangelists always call the city "Bethsaida," not "Julia" (its name when they wrote), evidence that they were working with early traditions and that they were not cavalier about the conservativeness of their sources? Do the traditions linked with this city antedate the renaming of the city in 30 C.E.? That is, Jesus visited the village called Bethsaida, but he never set foot in it when it became a city called Julia, since in 30 C.E. he was crucified in Jerusalem. The conservative nature of the Gospels at this point should be acknowledged.

Recognizing the Greek and Roman culture that was evident, along with Judaism, in Bethsaida may help us understand why the Greeks seeking to meet Jesus first find Philip, a disciple with a Greek name, who was "from Bethsaida in Galilee" (John 12:21). It is also interesting to note that Philip immediately goes to talk with Andrew, who also bore a Greek name and also was from Bethsaida (John 1:44). Subsequently, Philip and Andrew go to Jesus to speak to him about the Greeks who "wish to see Jesus" (John 12:21). Of course, the Evangelist ultimately shaped the narrative, but archaeology does help us understand the history in the story. However, if some issues are becoming clarified, others remain unclear. For example, why did Jesus curse Bethsaida (Matt 11:21; Luke 10:13)? The New Testament provides us with no answers.

Archaeological discoveries are essential as we endeavor to reconstruct the life and teachings of Jesus of Nazareth. Among the archaeological treasures recovered, the most important are the Dead Sea Scrolls. These are not copies of ancient writings; they are the ancient scrolls held by Jesus' contemporaries in ancient Palestine. It should be recognized that no longer will a purely literary approach be acceptable.

As we ponder this insight, one additional source of information is essential before any sensitive and in-depth attempt to reconstruct the life and teachings of Jesus of Nazareth. This source is topography and the Semitic culture alive now where Jesus lived and taught.[66] Specialists need to spend time in the so-called Holy Land, holding olives and olive seeds, sitting under olive trees, and thinking about the appropriate parable. They need to wander through the hills and observe shepherds with black goats and off-white sheep pastorally strolling tirelessly in a lunaresque landscape. They need to stand beside the Sea of Galilee and feel the wind whistling off the Golan Heights, pondering the plight of fishermen out on the lake.[67] They should wander around the remains of Herodian Jericho, thinking about the opulence there long ago, and stand within the large swimming pool in which Herod had the high priest drowned. They would do well to sit in one of the Qumran caves and think about the Torah and God's will lived out in the wilderness. Perhaps reflections will turn to the Qumran Essenes, who claimed to be in the wilderness because they heard the voice calling them to prepare the way of the Lord in the wilderness (Isa 40:3).[68] They might even sit at sunset in the Garden of Gethsemane and look down on the Old City of Jerusalem, philosophically thinking about the meaning of life and the views once observed by Jesus.

Any form of historical reconstruction is dependent on primary sources and *informed imagination*. Without controlling sources, imagination tends to concoct fables; without informed imagination, invaluable sources may lie lifeless. No stone talks — except within writings that are either poetic or apocalyptic. But with the skills of an archaeologist and a historian, a stone might be able to tell a palpable story. Thus it is imperative for the exegete and historian to feel the topographical landscape and the Semitic environment of the land. It is easy to comprehend why some gifted, archaeologically trained historians have rightly called topography "the fifth gospel."[69]

Any who would attempt to reconstruct the life and teachings of Jesus should spend ample time in Galilee and Jerusalem. It is helpful to hear the Semitic sounds of Arabs conversing or Jews talking. It is imperative to realize that logic is a foreign concept in the lives of those who live in Israel or Palestine. Since Jesus' native tongue was Aramaic and he probably read the Scriptures in Hebrew, it is wise to hear and learn languages in which there is no past, present, or future. In Semitics, time is bifurcated, not trifurcated, and time is conceived in terms of unfulfilled or fulfilled action. When one realizes this aspect of Semitics, it is obvious that much that has been written about Jesus' concept of time was informed only by Greek and Latin and modern languages derived from them. Scholars and others have written a virtual library of books seeking to discern if Jesus thought God's kingdom was future or present. When one realizes that he did not categorize his proclamations and parables in terms of the future and the present, we come much closer to the dynamic element in his teachings.

Finally, Semitic sounds are resonant and repetitive and so often connect thoughts and patterns of thought, thereby revealing the relationship among words. Hearing — and perhaps speaking — a Semitic language helps the Jesus researcher more accurately approximate Jesus' words and some of his *ipsissima vox*, or authentic voice.

M. A. K. Halliday and Brian K. Blount have demonstrated

that all interpreters of traditions are influenced by the context in which and out of which they write.[70] Allowing one's own context to be open and shaped by some of the Semitic world today in the land can significantly improve interpretation, imagination, and ultimately the reconstruction of Jesus' time and life.

I have tried to demonstrate that we have ten major categories of sources for seeking to understand and reconstruct Jesus' life and teachings. Eight sources are collections of literary documents that provide information about Jesus, either directly or indirectly. These are the New Testament — which deserves pride of place for being the singularly most important source — Josephus's writings, the New Testament Apocrypha and Pseudepigrapha, the Mishnah, the Old Testament Apocrypha, the Old Testament Pseudepigrapha, the Dead Sea Scrolls, and the Greek Magical Papyri. Now being recognized as essential for understanding Jesus and his time is the study of archaeological discoveries and sites and the topography and Semitic culture in the land today.

Methodology

Jesus of Nazareth is the most famous person in the history of Western culture. It is not surprising, therefore, that novelists and authors untrained in the study of early Judaism and Christian origins have written voluminously about him. Most of what has been written is worthless from a historian's point of view. Why? It is because the improper methodology was employed. Let me make a few comments about how to study Jesus historically.

First, we must comprehend that what Jesus did and said was remembered orally for decades, and this process continued into the second century and long after the compositions of the canonical gospels. Mark, Matthew, and Luke never knew Jesus. The Fourth Gospel contains the claim that it is based upon the account of an eyewitness, and it is possible that some truth may lie in this claim, as I tried to indicate, inter alia, in *The Beloved Disciple*.[71]

Second, reports in the Gospels of what Jesus said and did must be evaluated according to coherent criteria.[72] This is certainly not the place to discuss and defend the criteria for discerning Jesus' traditions within Jesus-traditions, that is, isolating what he probably said and did from what has been attributed to him in the intracanonical and extracanonical gospels.[73] While many scholars commence with assuming that a Jesus-tradition is inauthentic until proven authentic, I think that we should assume a tradition is authentic until evidence appears that undermines its authenticity. I take this position because of the intentionality of the texts; that is, within a few decades of Jesus' death his followers (some of whom may have been eyewitnesses) attributed the saying to him. I have no doubt that if we could ask his followers, "Should we take this saying of Jesus as a historical fact?" they would reply, "Certainly." In contrast to Hillel-traditions, which sometimes were finally written down more than five centuries after he lived, Jesus-traditions originated in and took a written form in the century in which he lived.[74] Learned persons and their communities claimed in the first century and even before 70 C.E. that Jesus had said and done what is recorded in Mark and the earliest sections of Matthew, Luke, and John. Jesus' earliest followers were often gifted and well trained. They were not poor, ignorant peasants or rustic fishermen, as earlier critics assumed. I am well aware that *the assumption of authenticity* will appear anathema to some critics, but I am convinced that we need to pay more heed to *the context* in which a Jesus-saying appears. Jesus' sayings were not transmitted only centuries after his time and in a social context that encouraged creative and misrepresentative sayings. His sayings were transmitted within a decade of his death, and within a somewhat controlled environment. The polemical setting in which his followers lived, and were beginning to write down what he had said, would have made it foolhardy for anyone to claim that Jesus had not been crucified and that Peter had not denied him. This assumption also allows for the recognition, because of overall context, that the Evangelists certainly did take incredible liberties in shaping the Jesus tradition.

Before waxing too optimistic and composing histories of Jesus that are too positivistic, we need to report that almost always suspicions about inauthenticity appear; that is, it soon becomes readily apparent to the attentive researcher that traditions about Jesus often arise after the belief in his resurrection had shaped the thinking of his followers. The transmitters of tradition and compilers of the Gospels were never interested first and foremost in giving us an uninterpreted life of Jesus. They proclaimed the one who had been the consummate proclaimer. We also have come to recognize that the human does not have the ability to present a life of someone without interpretation. Most of us would admit that, even if such an impossibility might be possible, we would not want to read it. It would be as dull and dead as most of the papyri and ostraca that I have studied. There is little interest for me in a saying like the report that "Qausyehab, crushed wheat: 6 *seah*, 1 *qab*."[75] I really have little interest in finding out who is "Qausyehab" and why it is important to report that he crushed some wheat. However, I am very interested in learning something significant about Jesus. And I do not want simple reports that he was able to crush some wheat. I need interpretation and insight from his own time. That request is precisely what we encounter when we read the Gospels.

I am convinced that the two most important criteria for authenticity are the criterion of dissimilarity to the Christology and theology of the members of the Palestinian Jesus movement and the criterion of embarrassment to his followers. That is, if a saying or act is dissimilar to his followers' way of thinking or embarrassing to them, then it most likely did not arise with them. Since it is attributed to Jesus, it may well have originated with him. A third major criterion is multiple attestation; that is, a saying or action attributed to Jesus preserved in two or more independent primary sources is more probably original to Jesus than if it were found in only one source. When we have successfully isolated such a saying or act, then we must allow for alteration — or editing — of Jesus' tradition.

It is thereby clear that a biography of Jesus is impossible.[76] As we search the sources for reliable traditions that may originate with him, we should always remember that *Mark,* whoever he was, *never knew Jesus.* That means he could not appeal to his own memory for clarifying when and where Jesus said or did something. The earliest Evangelist (perhaps) was forced to create an order for Jesus' life. Mark's task may be compared to the attempts of someone who had broken a woman's pearl necklace and was forced to put the pearls back in the original order. That is as impossible as it was for Mark to recreate the order of Jesus' traditions.

What is possible for us today? First, we must not let our own wishes and desires dictate methods or conclusions. If we ask honest questions, then we must honestly seek to answer them. That means being true to the questions without regard to any possible answer. Otherwise we deceive ourselves into thinking we are honest. If our method is not informed and honest, we become incapable of learning what are the most probable answers. I am convinced that a reliable portrait of Jesus is likely. We may not be able to present Jesus' authentic words (the so-called *ipsissima verba Jesu,*) but we can discuss what he probably intended to communicate to his followers and others who heard him. We will never be certain what Jesus may have intended by some of his actions, but we can be relatively certain that he did do some of the things attributed to him.

What then might be known historically about Jesus? And what can be related briefly? To answer this focused question succinctly, I shall present a list, with an indication of where the historical datum might be placed on the spectrum of probability, since the historian's approximation to certainty is a mere "highly probable." The spectrum is thence as follows (from the least to the most certain): barely conceivable, conceivable, possible, probable, and highly probable.

As I have already hinted, the intracanonical gospels took shape within decades of Jesus' death. They reflect the years in which *Jesus' traditions* — that is, the traditions that originated with him — evolved or developed into *Jesus-traditions* that reflected the need to proclaim the Proclaimer, as Bultmann and many New Testament specialists showed. Many of the most cherished traditions in the Jesus story were created by the needs of the Palestinian Jesus movement. They thus did not originate with Jesus and are fabricated Jesus-traditions (that is, words and actions illegitimately attributed to Jesus).

As David Friedrich Strauss pointed out in his massive work on Jesus that appeared in 1835, some of these Jesus-traditions are myths that developed out of three human perspectives. First, some originated as philosophical or theological truths. Second, others evolved from poetic imaginations. Third, some, perhaps many, were grounded in real historical events, and these were of such momentous importance that they are possible to relate only via myths. We commence, then, by looking at the legendary portrayal of Jesus and move towards the relatively reliable historical information about Jesus of Nazareth.

The Story

This section lists the legendary and perhaps mythological aspects of Jesus' life and teaching that are full of meaning christologically but probably did not happen historically as described. These aspects of the Jesus story were most likely composed to celebrate Jesus as the Christ or Son of God. In assessing these invaluable dimensions of the Jesus-traditions, we should remember that his followers were an insignificant sect that was persecuted, with some members even martyred, by the dominant priestly establishment in Jerusalem.[77] Moreover, there are truths in myths; in fact, truth often demands such a vehicle.

The virgin birth derives from mythological traditions found in Jewish as well as Roman traditions. It is not found in Mark or John.

The genealogies are the creation of scribes. It is conceivable that there may be some historical facts behind them. They are not found in Mark or John.

It is unlikely that wisemen attended Jesus' birth. This story is found only in Matthew.

Luke's unique story of the singing of a heavenly chorus is pure embellishment.

It seems relatively certain that Jesus' exodus from Egypt, in Matthew, was created out of the conviction that Scripture so indicated he was God's son. It is unique to Matthew and reflects his narrative style and theological tendency.

The story of Satan's temptation is most likely fabricated out of ancient biblical traditions. Since it is placed in the wilderness (Mark 1:12), it might be a theological means of narrating how Jesus was *prepared* for his lifework, since in biblical theology "wilderness" denotes the place of preparation.

Legends and myths probably created the account of Jesus' speaking with wisdom in the temple as a youth.[78] The story is unique to Luke.

Mythological reflections have created the idea that Jesus turned water into wine. The story is found only in John, and the account does not describe any action by Jesus that would cause water to become wine.

Christological reflections have led to the contention that Jesus walked on the water. The purpose of the story is to draw attention to Jesus and is thus motivated by Christology and not history.

The Transfiguration serves to elevate Jesus' status and is mythological Christology. That is, the motive behind the story is not history; it is Christology and celebration.

It is improbable that Jesus raised Jairus's daughter, the widow of Nain's son, and Lazarus from the dead. Such stories elevate Jesus and seem to reflect the early kerygma (proclamation) that stressed his divine or messianic qualities.

Christology has created the account of Jesus' calming of the storm and sea. Again, the motive is to proclaim Jesus as Lord of the cosmos.

It is improbable that Jesus established the institution of the eucharist as described in the Synoptics. The liturgies in early Judaism and in the Palestinian Jesus movement certainly helped shape this account.

Beliefs in Jesus as the charismatic miracle worker probably created the account of his feeding four thousand and five thousand. Surely, the motive is not history; it is Christology.

The needs of the confessing community seem to have originated the accounts in which Jesus predicts he will be crucified.
If Jesus predicted his crucifixion, then why do his disciples
seem so ill-prepared for the event? The Gospels at this point
were clearly written from the Crucifixion back to the early years
of Jesus.

Unbridled enthusiasm has led to the expansionistic descriptions of Jesus' resurrection appearances (esp. John 21).
These accounts clearly reflect the resurrection faith of Jesus' followers. The resurrection faith of Jesus' followers was one of the
main catalysts for proclaiming the "good news" and writing the
Gospels.

Possible Aspects of His Life and Teaching

In contrast to the former category, some aspects of Jesus' life are
more reliable historically. Historians have successfully shown
that numerous sayings and actions of Jesus are less part of the
Gospel narrative and more a dimension of Jesus' history. Here
are the most important ones in my opinion:

Jesus may have been born in Bethlehem, despite Matthew
and Luke's use of Scripture to prove it.

Jesus was most likely related to the Baptist and could have
been of priestly lineage.

Jesus may have been a Davidad. At least three strata preserve this tradition.

He possibly went to Jerusalem for his bar mitzvah. He was
very Jewish.

Jesus may not have been a "carpenter," and his parables
connect him more with farming and fishing. This conclusion
derives from studying all four Gospels.

It is possible Jesus may have worn a *tsitsith* (ציצית; cf. Num
15:39: "You shall have it as a fringe") and conceivably a phylactery. The woman with a hemorrhage seemed to have touched
Jesus' fringed garment (*kraspedou*; Matt 9:20; Luke 8:44; cf. Mark
6:56 and Matt 14:36). If he wore a *tsitsith,* then he most likely
wore a phylactery, at least on special religious occasions.

It is conceivable, perhaps likely, that Jesus spent all night in prayer dedicated to God (Luke 6:12; *dianuktereuōn*). The habit is clearly stated in Luke, reflected in Mark, and explains the sleeping disciples in Gethsemane on Jesus' last night. It is possible that Jesus had a messianic self-understanding, and it is conceivable that he may have considered himself the designated Messiah. These aspects of his life permeate virtually all sources.

Despite the embellishments in the triumphal entry, Jesus may have entered Jerusalem on an animal and with public fanfare. The action makes sense in terms of our study of pilgrimages and sociological studies of Jerusalem at Passover time in Jerusalem.[79]

Some of the Sanhedrin were perhaps behind his arrest, but they may not have contemplated his death. The evidence is again well attested by the Gospels and comments by Josephus.

It is only barely conceivable that Jesus contemplated a place for gentiles in his community, and the stories about the Syrophoenician woman and the centurion may indicate some change in his attitude toward gentiles.

It is barely conceivable that Jesus predicted the temple's destruction due to hostility against Rome.

Relatively Certain Aspects of His Life and Teaching

Thanks to careful research by scholars in Germany, France, Sweden, England, Israel, and the United States especially and since the end of the seventeenth century, we can report that some aspects of Jesus' life and teaching are relatively certain. Space demands succinctness, and (usually) no reasons for the conclusion can be given.

Jesus was born in Palestine, probably in or near Nazareth. He was never called Jesus of Bethlehem but frequently Jesus of Nazareth.

Nothing can be known with any probability about the years before his public ministry. The intracanonical gospels and Josephus make no mention of his childhood or youth.

Jesus was probably not born into a poverty-stricken, or even poor, family. If he knew Scripture as well as his contemporaries claimed, he must have spent some time studying, which would not have been possible for a peasant.

Unlike Polybius, Philo, Paul, and Josephus, Jesus did not travel widely. It is highly improbable that he left "the land of Israel," or ancient Palestine.

Jesus joined John the Baptizer, who was probably his teacher. The traditions preserved in the intracanonical gospels, and especially Mark and John, have proved to be relatively reliable regarding Jesus' relation with John the Baptizer.

If the Fourth Gospel preserves reliable historical information about Jesus' early ministry, he led a baptist movement for an indeterminate amount of time.

Jesus was baptized by John the Baptizer. The embarrassment throughout the New Testament about this episode confirms its historicity.

Jesus probably interpreted Isa 40:3 differently from John the Baptizer and the Qumranites and their teacher. Unlike them, he did not think a voice had called him *into* the wilderness. For Jesus, the voice was calling *from* the wilderness.

Jesus left the wilderness and taught on the outskirts of cities and villages.

Jesus was charismatic, an eloquent speaker, and powerfully influenced many Jews. We learn this historical datum from studying the Gospels and Josephus.

Jesus was gifted as a storyteller and poet.

He spoke with uncommon authority and directly, without citing authorities.[80]

He was neither a student of Hillel nor of the Righteous Teacher of Qumran.

Jesus was politically antirevolutionary, and he was not a Zealot.[81] Yet it is absurd to assume, or to conclude, that Jesus had no political agenda.[82] After all, John the Baptist was beheaded by a Herodian ruler, and Jesus was put to death by the command of a Roman governor.

Jesus was often invited to dinners and knew the joy of companionship and wine.

Some Pharisees admired him, sought his company, and probably warned him about problems.

Other Pharisees, especially those from Judea and Jerusalem, sought to entrap him.

He taught in Galilee and Judea and probably in Samaria.

He performed miracles, notably the healing miracles, because his opponents affirmed that point by explaining how he was able to do miracles. They said he was possessed of a devil or was the Devil. For the Evangelists, Jesus' miracles revealed that he had been sent to them by God.[83]

Jesus spoke primarily Aramaic, but he knew Hebrew, Greek, and a little Latin.

The Beatitudes probably derive ultimately from Jesus because a form strikingly similar to them has now been found in the Dead Sea Scrolls; that is to say, this manner of speaking was not created by his followers.

Jesus' favorite means of speaking was in parables, and they ring true to his intentionality that God's kingdom was now dawning in the present. His parables are closest to those of the Pharisees, for only Jesus and the Pharisees used parables as a means of teaching.[84] We derive the conclusion that Jesus' favorite form of teaching was the parable from the Synoptics and the *Gospel of Thomas*.

Jesus probably quoted only Scripture that is now canonized, but he was influenced by other sacred Jewish writings.

He was obsessed with God.

He did not proclaim himself and was emphatically monotheistic.

Jesus' sayings are often characterized by difficult demands and assumptions that run counter to normal human, especially family, relationships.[85]

His essential message was the proclamation of the dawning of God's kingdom [= God's rule], as we know from research upon the synoptic Gospels and the *Gospel of Thomas*.

Jesus' message was fundamentally eschatological; that is, his parables and teachings and the prayer he taught contain the perspective that the present time is impregnated with the power of the end of time.

Jesus elevated the concept of love and made it central in his teachings; he even seems to have taught that his followers should love their enemies. Ironically, perhaps, the best elucidation of this point is by the Jew David Flusser in his chapter on "love" in the revision of his *Jesus*.[86] We obtain this insight by studying all four intracanonical gospels, the *Gospel of Thomas*, and the letters of Paul.

Some of his statements indicate that he probably thought the kingdom would dawn in his lifetime (Mark 9:1).

Jesus probably did not know the precise time of the end of time (Mark 13:32).

Jesus demanded absolute commitment to God's rule. This point readily appears from the study of the intracanonical gospels and the *Gospel of Thomas*.

He probably taught a form of the Lord's Prayer. I am persuaded that the versions in Matthew and Luke derive from two independent sources.[87]

Jesus most likely thought he was "the Son of God," but it is far from clear what that meant to him. This title is found in his parables and in other early strata, including the parable of the wicked tenant farmers in two independent sources, Mark and the *Gospel of Thomas*. Jesus' understanding of himself as "God's Son" must not be confused with the Nicene formula.[88]

Unlike the Qumranites, Jesus had low, even no, social barriers and virtually no requirements for "admission" into his group.

At least during portions of his ministry, he included only Jews, and it is barely conceivable, at best, that he thought his mission also included gentiles.

Some Samaritans probably admired Jesus and may have affirmed that he was a Samaritan (John 4; 8:48–49).

Jesus included women and probably broke with many in his culture about women's status in society. This conclusion derives from studying the intracanonical gospels, especially the Gospel of John.[89]

Jesus probably never broke the sabbath according to the Torah, but he certainly broke the sabbath laws developed by some of the Jewish groups or sects.

Jesus was a very devout Jew. In fact, he was more Jewish than Philo, who mixed Jewish traditions in the caldron of Greek ideals and myths, and Josephus, who explained Jewish theology as if it were like Greek philosophy.

Jesus was probably never married.[90]

It is highly probable that Jesus chose twelve disciples; otherwise, it is inexplicable why his followers would have created that tradition and placed Judas within it. Thus, it is possible that Jesus had more than a mere spiritual revolution in mind. This conclusion derives from the application of the criterion of embarrassment.

It seems likely that James and John requested thrones beside Jesus. The embarrassment of the tradition is obvious when one sees how Matthew shifts Mark's statement from them to their mother.

Jesus did not found the "Church," but he probably called into being a special eschatological group. This conclusion is apparent from a study of the intracanonical gospels, the *Gospel of Thomas,* and Josephus.

Jesus' disciples seemed to misunderstand him, and Peter most likely denied him. Again, multiple attestation tends to prove this conclusion.

Jesus' involvement with the Baptist and Jesus' crucifixion suggest that some leaders saw him as a political person and threat.

Jesus probably developed a view of purity that was diametrically opposed to that in Jerusalem. It is also evident that the Galilean Jesus intentionally — and thereby polemically — opposed the Jerusalem establishment.

He was tested, even persecuted, by scribes sent out from the priests in authority in Jerusalem. This probability is well attested.

He taught in the temple and admired it. He may have called it "my Father's house." There is no evidence that his followers created such traditions.

Jesus probably revered most aspects of the cult in the temple.

He went to Jerusalem in order to fulfill the injunction of

the Torah and to celebrate Passover. That seems to be an obvious inference from a study of the intracanonical gospels and a perception of Jesus' Jewishness.

Jesus probably overturned the tables of the money changers, and it is conceivable that he was protesting some excesses of the cult and the excessive demands for ritual purity. This interpretation makes best sense of all the data we possess, especially the Jewish writings from the time of Jesus.

It is highly probable that he thought he might be murdered. He seems to think he may be stoned outside Jerusalem, as had the miracle worker named Honi, but it is unlikely that he ever contemplated he would be crucified. This insight seems to derive from the texts that suggest he had an intuition he might be stoned and from a study of the four gospels and the *Gospel of Thomas*.[91]

It is possible, and maybe probable, that Jesus feared the coming danger and most likely death when he prayed before his arrest, looking down on the temple from the Garden of Gethsemane.

It is not clear that Judas "betrayed" him. The witness of the Fourth Gospel must be neither ignored nor exaggerated. Since the authorities obviously were able to recognize Jesus, Judas did not betray Jesus' identity, but then what did he betray?

During his last supper, Jesus probably celebrated a meal with Passover in mind and said something similar to that found in Paul (1 Corinthians 11) while stressing the dawning of God's rule and the importance of the Twelve within it.[92] We know this from a study of the traditions in Paul's authentic letters and the four intracanonical gospels.

Jesus was condemned to die from crucifixion by Pilate, who was most likely staying in Herod's Palace in the Upper City of Jerusalem, as the three names *praetorium* (the governor's residence), *lithostroton* (the large public elegant stone pavement), and *gabbatha* (the Hebrew equivalent of the Greek *lithostroton*) signify.[93]

He was tied or nailed to the cross by Roman soldiers. We obtain this information from the four intracanonical gospels and from early traditions in the *Gospel of Peter*.

Jesus seems to have died confused, and his last words were most likely, "My God, my God, why...?" The criterion of embarrassment helps at this point.

After Jesus' crucifixion his followers fled. Some probably went back to Galilee (John 21). Many most likely looked back on his life and admitted they "had hoped" (Emmaus story). The embarrassment of his followers and multiple attestation lift this point to a very high level of probability.

It is possible, and perhaps probable, that Jesus was raised by God, as Jews like Lapide explain and Flusser contemplate.[94] It also makes sense in light of early Jewish theology. It is well attested in the intracanonical and extracanonical gospels, Paul, and other very early sources.

Mary Magdalene, not Peter, was probably the first to see him after the Resurrection. The criterion of embarrassment and the tendencies of the sources help us comprehend this probability.

It has been difficult to resist the temptation to turn each entry in these three lists into a separate lecture. The urge to do so is especially strong with those that are new and have appeared unexpectedly from my own research.[95]

It is apparent to the informed reader that in the contemporary debate I side with scholars like the conservative Protestant clergyman N. T. Wright,[96] the liberal or secular Protestant E. P. Sanders,[97] the Roman Catholic John Meier,[98] the multinational Jew Geza Vermes,[99] and the Israeli Jew David Flusser.[100] From different perspectives we all are convinced that scholars today have far more reliable historical knowledge about what Jesus said and did than our teachers had been willing to admit.

What does Jesus research have to do with faith? Perhaps nothing. It is not because of something lacking in our Bibles that scholars are inquisitive. That quality of the human is never to be squelched by anyone, especially the pious ecclesiastics. Unfortunately, some in the so-called third quest are still seeking to find a Lord they can follow and admire. It is a pity that Luke T. Johnson, whom I deeply respect, has given some readers of his *The Real Jesus* the impression that historical research takes a back seat to theological study. I feel compelled to differ from Johnson when he concludes that the "Jesus of the Gospels" should be sufficient for all "who declare a desire for religious truth, and theological integrity, and honest history."[101] The honest search for history must never be encased within, or constricted by, a canon that appreciably postdates the century in which Jesus lived.

The feeling of a historian when confronted by the task of discerning what is authentic and what is apocryphal is one of frustration and humility. How can we expect or hope to reconstruct first-century Judaism and Jesus' place within it when we fail to be able to answer such simple questions as these: Who were Mary Magdalene and Judas, and what were their motives in joining Jesus' group? According to our extant sources, why did Jesus never discuss messianology with his disciples, and why did they never ask him what he thought about the Messiah? Why did Jesus apparently prefer calling God Father? What had he been doing before he joined John the Baptizer's group?

Our work is fraught with perplexing problems. We have virtually no knowledge regarding the authors of the Gospels of Matthew, Mark, Luke, John, and Thomas. We do not know what sources they used or how reliable these were historically. We have not one fragment of a New Testament document from the first century.[102]

Conclusion

During much of this century it has been vogue to report in the academy and in the seminary — but certainly never in the Church — that we know practically nothing about Jesus. This was the conclusion of Bultmann and his influential school in Germany and America. About all that could be known was the sheer isolated fact that Jesus had existed and been crucified. Notice these words of Bultmann: "I do indeed think that we can now know almost nothing concerning the life and personality of Jesus, since the early Christian sources show no interest in either, are moreover fragmentary and often legendary; and other sources about Jesus do not exist."[103] When I have cited this passage from Bultmann, scholars have told me I misquoted Bultmann; yet, he made this claim, and it did influence his students.

I cannot agree with Bultmann that the "early Christian sources show no interest" in Jesus' life, while I would agree that they were not interested in his personality — that is, in the modern psychological meaning of the term. Bultmann developed this position before the discovery of the Nag Hammadi Codices and the Dead Sea Scrolls, and so the question arises what difference they make. For Bultmann, they did not make a difference. For me, they make a significant difference. I would stress two points. First, among the Nag Hammadi Codices, the *Gospel of Thomas* is clearly a source for Jesus research. And second, while the Dead Sea Scrolls are not "sources about Jesus" — none of the Dead Sea Scrolls mentions Jesus or any of his disciples — they are "a source" for this research, providing terms, perspectives, and methods of interpreting Scripture that help us understand him.[104]

While a moratorium on the quest of the historical Jesus is the hallmark of the Bultmannian school, yet we should not forget the inconsistencies in some of Bultmann's work. While he did stress that faith requires only the givenness of Jesus (the *dass*), he did write a major book on Jesus. In this book he argued that we can know quite a lot about Jesus' teaching concerning the coming of God's kingdom and about the will of God.

Since 1980 "Jesus research" is the technical term that defines the work of some scholars, such as E. P. Sanders, John Meier, and myself, who are not primarily interested in, or blinded by, theological concerns. In contrast, the term "the third quest of the historical Jesus" characterizes the work of some New Testament scholars, like Marcus J. Borg, who are seeking to discern Jesus' meaning for Christian faith.[105] While the distinction between historians and theologians in Jesus research was evident in the '80s, it is not so clear today, as more and more scholars are interested in the study of the historical Jesus in terms of secular history and the theology of the Evangelists.

Of course, I am also interested in theology, but I will not

allow theological issues to contaminate my historiography. Literary and nonliterary studies have given us many valuable insights into the historical Jesus. Jesus is not some unknown person hidden behind the confessions in the Gospels.[106] Along with many more scholars I have concluded that we know more about Jesus than about almost any other first-century Jew, with the exceptions of Paul and Josephus, both of whom — unlike Jesus — wrote numerous epistles or books. We certainly know far more about Jesus than his near contemporary Hillel.[107]

Some Christians — especially Roman Catholics — are shocked to learn that Jesus actually lived and was a Jew from Galilee.[108] Others find such conclusions difficult to relate to their contention that Christianity is pure theology untainted by historical issues. For Jews, Jesus research, let alone the quest, can be irrelevant. For others, like David Flusser in his *Jesus* (1997, 1998), Jesus' message and life are powerful and perhaps the greatest moments in the history of religions.

Christianity is a historical religion. Christian belief is never only an idea, as D. F. Strauss at times indicated. Christian faith is founded in a real person who, as we know from the Fourth Gospel, was flesh and blood. Jesus did not merely take on flesh; he was flesh. Jesus' earthiness undergirds Christology. Such points so characterized an earlier Faith and Scholarship Colloquy that they were published under the title *Earthing Christologies* and edited by Walter P. Weaver and myself.

Now, thanks to the Jewish documents that come from Jesus' time, and especially to the Dead Sea Scrolls, which his contemporaries once held before I and others touched them, we can more adequately imagine Jesus in his first-century Jewish context. We may imagine him sauntering through the fields of Galilee or teaching in the temple, debating with Essenes, Pharisees, scribes, and even Sadducees, as well as many others. Now, thanks to the realia provided by archaeologists, we can imagine the garments and sandals he and his contemporaries wore.

What does all of this ultimately have to do with faith? No one can report for another. Each must seek to obtain personal answers. It takes studying, reading, meditating, and praying. I personally profit from pondering the beauty in Paul's claim that Christ has freed us for freedom (Gal 5:1). I disagree with Bultmann that Jesus is the presupposition of New Testament theology.[109] For me, as with Leonhard Goppelt,[110] Jesus' message is the beginning of New Testament theology. He, and not his followers, seemed to have combined such highly theological concepts as "the Son of Man" and "the Messiah" — although I am also persuaded that a Jewish genius before him may well have already made this association.[111] Not only history but archaeology and sociology are important to comprehend the historical Jesus.[112] As for the members of the Palestinian Jesus movement, so for many of us Christians, Jesus is the one who enables God to be present in our midst — and in an awesome way.

Notes

1. I agree with James D. G. Dunn, who argues in his helpful book on Jesus, "Christians *should* want to know the truth — even when it hurts." Dunn, *The Evidence for Jesus* (Philadelphia: Westminster, 1985) xiii.

2. For guides to publications, see Craig A. Evans, *Life of Jesus Research: An Annotated Bibliography,* rev. ed., New Testament Tools and Studies 24 (Leiden: Brill, 1996); and W. E. Mills, *Periodical Literature on Christ and the Gospels* (Leiden: Brill, 1997). The notes that follow are highly selected, and the temptation to cite the thousands of books on Jesus in my library is great. This series is not the place for such documentation. My indebtedness to other specialists in Jesus research is obvious. The notes that remain are to provide guidance when such is deemed necessary.

3. For an authoritative assessment of current research on the historical Jesus, see Bruce Chilton and Craig A. Evans, eds., *Studying the Historical Jesus: Evaluations of the State of Current Research,* New Testament Tools and Study 19 (Leiden: Brill, 1994).

4. This conclusion is the result of my research as Lady Davis Professor in the History Department, Hebrew University, Jerusalem. I have not yet published it.

5. In my judgment this search for certainty within a world of historical probability undermined much of the superb work of Norman Perrin, esp. in his *Rediscovering the Teaching of Jesus,* New Testament Library (London: SCM, 1967).

6. N. T. Wright coined the new phase of research "the Third

Quest" of the historical Jesus. See his important *Jesus and the Victory of God* (London: SPCK, 1996) esp. 83.

7. J. H. Charlesworth and W. P. Weaver, *Images of Jesus Today*, Faith and Scholarship Colloquies 2 (Valley Forge, Pa.: Trinity Press International, 1994).

8. E. P. Sanders, *Jesus and Judaism* (Philadelphia: Fortress, 1985) 2. Also, see Sanders, *The Historical Figure of Jesus* (New York and London: Allen Lane Penguin Press, 1993, 1995).

9. Samuel Byrskog who has focused on Matthew 23:8, for example, has shown that Jesus' sayings were passed on by "a careful and controlled transmission process." See his *Jesus the Only Teacher*, Coniectanea biblica, New Testament Series 24 (Stockholm: Almqvist and Wiksell, 1994) 401.

10. David Hill, *New Testament Prophecy* (Atlanta: John Knox, 1979); and David Edward Aune, *Prophecy in Early Christianity and the Ancient Mediterranean World* (Grand Rapids: Eerdmans, 1983).

11. The quotations are from Aune, *Prophecy in Early Christianity*, 245.

12. Far too typical today is the claim by John Shelby Spong, "I do not look to the Fourth Gospel for historic accuracy. No life of Jesus can be constructed from this volume." See Spong, *This Hebrew Lord: A Bishop's Search for the Authentic Jesus* (San Francisco: HarperSanFrancisco, 1993) 141. Bargil Pixner bases his study of Jesus in Jerusalem on the Fourth Gospel. He is one of the most knowledgeable archaeologists on tradition and excavations in Jerusalem, especially Zion. See his *With Jesus in Jerusalem* (Rosh Pina, Israel: Corazin Publishing, 1996).

13. See esp. Barbara Aland and Kurt Aland and others, *Novum Testamentum Graece*, 27th ed. (Stuttgart: Deutsche Bibelgesellschaft, 1993); and R. Swanson, ed., *New Testament Greek Manuscripts*, 4 vols. (Sheffield: Sheffield Academic Press; Pasadena, Calif.: William Carey International University Press, 1995).

14. For a monumental publication of Hellenistic attitudes to Jews, see Menahem Stern, *Greek and Latin Authors on Jews and Judaism*, 3 vols. (Jerusalem: Israel Academy of Sciences and Humanities, 1976–84).

15. These are easily located under the name of the translator: H. St. J. Thackeray; for example, Thackeray, trans., *Josephus: The Life of Apion*, Loeb Classical Library 186 (Cambridge and London: Harvard University Press, 1976). For Whiston's translation, see William Whiston, trans., *The Works of Josephus: Complete and Unabridged* (Peabody, Mass.: Hendrickson, 1996). (Whiston lived from 1667 to 1752.)

16. James H. Charlesworth, *Jesus within Judaism: New Light from Exciting Archaeological Discoveries*, Anchor Bible Reference Library (Garden City, N.Y.: Doubleday, 1988) 77–102.

17. For a divergent assessment, see John P. Meier, who disparages

the New Testament apocryphal documents. See his otherwise magisterial work *A Marginal Jew*, 3 vols. (Garden City, N.Y.: Doubleday, 1991, 1994, and not yet completed) 1:112–66. For a very positive assessment of the New Testament Apocrypha, see Helmut Koester's *Introduction to the New Testament*, 2 vols. (Philadelphia: Fortress, 1982). See the more recent editions.

18. John Dominic Crossan, *The Cross That Spoke: The Origins of the Passion Narrative* (San Francisco: Harper, 1988): H. Koester, *Ancient Christian Gospels* (Philadelphia: Trinity Press International, 1990).

19. Also see James H. Charlesworth, *Authentic Apocrypha*, The Dead Sea Scrolls and Christian Origins Library 2 (N. Richland Hills, Tex.: Bibal Press, 1998). For other books by Crossan, see his *Four Other Gospels* (Minneapolis, Chicago, and New York: Seabury, 1985); *The Historical Jesus: The Life of a Mediterranean Jewish Peasant* (San Francisco: HarperSanFrancisco, 1991); *The Essential Jesus* (San Francisco: HarperSanFrancisco, 1995); *Jesus: A Revolutionary Biography* (San Francisco: HarperSanFrancisco, 1995); *Who Killed Jesus?* (San Francisco: HarperSanFrancisco, 1995); *Who Is Jesus? Answers to Your Questions about the Historical Jesus* (New York: HarperPaperbacks, 1996).

20. Charlesworth and Evans, in Chilton and Evans, *Studying the Historical Jesus*, 479–533.

21. See esp. Bruce D. Chilton, "The Gospel according to Thomas as a Source of Jesus' Teaching," in *The Jesus Tradition outside the Gospels*, ed. David Wenham, Gospel Perspectives 5 (Sheffield: JSOT Press, 1984), 155–75.

22. See James H. Charlesworth, "Review Article," *Princeton Theological Seminary Bulletin*, n.s., 17 (1996) 399–403.

23. Wilhelm Schneemelcher and R. McL. Wilson, eds., *New Testament Apocrypha*, 2 vols., rev. ed. (Louisville: Westminster/John Knox, 1991–92).

24. J. K. Elliott, *The Apocryphal New Testament* (Oxford: Clarendon, 1993).

25. Koester, *Ancient Christian Gospels*.

26. The model of Jerusalem during the time of Jesus is worth seeing; see M. Avi-Yonah, *Pictorial Guide to the Model of Ancient Jerusalem at the Time of the Second Temple*, 2d ed. (Herzlia, Israel: Palphot, [1998?]).

27. Herbert Danby, trans., *The Mishnah* (Oxford: Oxford University Press, 1933); and Jacob Neusner, trans., *The Mishnah* (New Haven and London: Yale University Press, 1988). Also important is the other collection of early Jewish traditions called the Tosephta; it has been translated by Neusner.

28. Among the many books, see esp. David R. Catchpole, *The Quest for Q* (Edinburgh: T. & T. Clark, 1993).

29. A seminal work, now dated, in the search for the Signs

Source is Robert T. Fortna's *The Gospel of Signs*, Society for New Testament Studies Monograph Series 11 (Cambridge: Cambridge University Press, 1970).

30. The best historical atlas of Jerusalem is Dan Bahat's *The Illustrated Atlas of Jerusalem*, with Chaim T. Rubinstein, trans. Shelomo Ketko (Jerusalem: Carta, 1996).

31. See, e.g., W. A. Meeks and others, eds., *The Harper Collins Study Bible: New Revised Standard Version* (New York: HarperCollins, 1993).

32. For further reflections, see James H. Charlesworth, *The Old Testament Pseudepigrapha and the New Testament: Prolegomena for the Study of Christian Origins* (Harrisburg, Pa.: Trinity Press International, 1998).

33. James H. Charlesworth, ed., *The Old Testament Pseudepigrapha*, 2 vols., Anchor Bible Reference Library (Garden City, N.Y.: Doubleday, 1983 and 1985 [and reprinted]).

34. Since in English, in contrast to German, "apocalyptic" is properly an adjective, we need another term to convey what is meant by the German noun *Apokalyptik*. Thus, "apocalypsology" denotes Jewish apocalyptic reflections and thoughts.

35. Jesus was clearly influenced by Jewish eschatology. Although Albert Schweitzer tended to overstate this case, he was instrumental in establishing this insight in the study of Jesus. See Schweitzer, *The Quest of the Historical Jesus: A Critical Study of Its Progress from Reimarus to Wrede*, trans. W. Montgomery (New York: Macmillan, 1964 [original German appeared in 1906]).

36. The best one-volume collection of Jewish texts essential for understanding Jesus in his time has been published recently by Lawrence H. Schiffman; see his *Texts and Traditions: A Source Reader for the Study of Second Temple and Rabbinic Judaism* (Hoboken, N.J.: KTAV, 1998). Three other collections containing non-Jewish texts that are important for understanding Jesus in his time are C. K. Barrett, *The New Testament Background: Writings from Ancient Greece and the Roman Empire That Illuminate Christian Origins*, 2d ed. (San Francisco: HarperSanFrancisco, 1989); Everett Ferguson, *Backgrounds of Early Christianity*, 2d ed. (Grand Rapids: Eerdmans, 1993); and M. Eugene Boring, Klaus Berger, and Carsten Colpe, eds., *Hellenistic Commentary to the New Testament* (Nashville: Abingdon, 1995).

37. See, e.g., James H. Charlesworth, ed., *The Rule of the Community and Related Documents*, Princeton Theological Seminary Dead Sea Scrolls Project 1 (Tübingen: Mohr [Siebeck]; Louisville: Westminster/John Knox, 1994).

38. Geza Vermes, trans., *The Complete Dead Sea Scrolls in English* (New York: Penguin, 1997).

39. Morton Smith, *Jesus the Magician* (San Francisco: Harper,

1978). For a sane review of magical influences on Jesus, see J. M. Hull, *Hellenistic Magic and the Synoptic Tradition,* Studies in Biblical Theology 28 (London and Naperville, Ill.: A. R. Allenson, 1974).

40. The animus against the term "magic" by many experts is unfortunate. We should heed Max Weber's insight that "elements of 'divine worship,' prayer and sacrifice, have their origin in magic." See J. Weber, *The Sociology of Religion,* trans. Ephraim Fischoff (Boston: Beacon, 1963 [the German original appeared in 1922]) 26.

41. I develop this thought in "Solomon and Jesus: The Son of David in Ante-Markan Traditions (Mk 10:47)," in *Biblical and Humane,* ed. Linda Bennett Elder and others (Atlanta: Scholars, 1996) 125–51.

42. Hans Dieter Betz, *The Greek Magical Papyri in Translation Including the Demotic Spells* (Chicago and London: University of Chicago Press, 1986; 2d ed. with updated bibliography, 1996).

43. Still valuable, but dated, is Jack Finegan, *The Archeology of the New Testament: The Life of Jesus and the Beginning of the Early Church* (Princeton: Princeton University Press, 1969). For the best collection of informed summaries of archaeological work, according to sites, see Ephraim Stern, ed., *The New Encyclopedia of Archaeological Excavations in the Holy Land,* 4 vols. (New York: Simon and Schuster, 1993).

44. When visiting Jerusalem, one should walk the walls of Jerusalem and look out and within, obtaining a personal definition of "Jerusalem." See Roni Ellenblum and Amnon Ramon, *The Walls of Jerusalem: A Guide to the Ramparts Walking Tour* (Jerusalem: Yad Izhak Ben-Zvi, 1995).

45. A good starting point would be to study the chapters in L. I. Levine, ed., *The Galilee in Late Antiquity* (New York and Jerusalem: Jewish Theological Seminary of America; Cambridge, Mass., and London: Harvard University Press, 1992). Also insightful is Sean Freyne, *Galilee, Jesus, and the Gospels: Literary Approaches and Historical Investigations* (Philadelphia: Fortress, 1988).

46. The best one-volume collection of studies on the Samaritans is Alan D. Crown, ed., *The Samaritans* (Tübingen: Mohr [Siebeck], 1989).

47. See the works listed under Jerusalem in the previous pages.

48. John J. Rousseau and Rami Arav, *Jesus and His World: An Archaeological and Cultural Dictionary* (Minneapolis: Fortress, 1995).

49. The works in this area are too numerous to list. One is singularly helpful for the beginner to "feel" life in first-century Galilee. It is Gerd Theissen, *The Shadow of the Galilean: The Quest of the Historical Jesus in Narrative Form,* trans. John Bowden (Philadelphia: Fortress, 1987). Also, see Theissen, *Histoire sociale du christianisme primitif,* Le monde de la Bible 33 (Geneva: Labor et Fides, 1996).

50. A very elementary book that helps the beginner ponder the

realia of life during the time of Jesus is Peter Connolly's *Living in the Time of Jesus of Nazareth* (Oxford: Oxford University Press, 1983).

51. The perfume may be purchased in the Israel Museum, Jerusalem. It is called "Abishag: Biblical Bouquet. Eau de Parfum." I was thrilled when the name I suggested for the perfume was accepted by the Israel authorities.

52. Yaakou Meshorer, *Ancient Jewish Coinage*, 2 vols. (New York: Amphora, 1982); *City-Coins of Eretz-Israel and the Decapolis in the Roman Period* (Jerusalem: Israel Museum, 1985); *The Coinage of Aelia Capitolina* (Jerusalem: Israel Museum, 1989); Y. Meshorer and S. Qedar, *The Coinage of Samaria in the Fourth Century BCE* (Jerusalem: Numismatic Fine Arts International, 1991). Also see the following: David R. Sear, *Roman Coins and Their Values*, rev. ed. (London: Seaby, 1988); *Greek Coins and Their Values*, 2 vols. (London: Seaby, 1978, 1994); Leo Mildenberg, ed., *The Abraham Bromberg Collection of Jewish Coins*, 2 vols. (Beverly Hills, Calif.: Superior Galleries; Zürich: Bank Leu Numismatics, 1991–92); Ewald Junge, *The Seaby Coin Encyclopaedia*, rev. ed. (London: Batsford, 1994); Kenneth W. Harl, *Coinage in the Roman Economy: 300 B.C. to A.D. 700* (Baltimore and London: Johns Hopkins University Press, 1996); David Hendin with Herbert Kreindler, *Guide to Biblical Coins*, 3d ed. (New York: Amphora, 1996); Larry J. Kreitzer, *Striking New Images: Roman Imperial Coinage and the New Testament World*, Journal for the Study of the New Testament, Supplement Series 134 (Sheffield: Sheffield Academic Press, 1996). Very helpful is Tyll Kroha's *Grosses Lexikon der Numismatik* (Gütersloh: Bertelsmann, 1997).

53. See the popular work entitled *An Ancient Boat Discovered in the Sea of Galilee* (Jerusalem: Israel Department of Antiquities and Museums, 1988); and Shelley Wachsmann, *The Excavations of an Ancient Boat in the Sea of Galilee (Lake Kinneret)*, Atiqot 19 (Jerusalem: Israel Antiquities Authority, 1990).

54. A popular and reliable discussion of Caesarea Maritima during the time of Jesus can be found in Kenneth G. Holum and others, eds., *King Herod's Dream: Caesarea on the Sea* (New York and London: Norton, 1988). Also, see Lee I. Levine, *Roman Caesarea*, Qedem 2 (Jerusalem: Israel Exploration Society, 1975); and Lee I. Levine and Ehud Netzer, *Excavations at Caesarea Maritima 1975, 1976, 1979 — Final Report*, Qedem 21 (Jerusalem: Israel Exploration Society, 1986).

55. See esp. the following popular booklets: Stanislao Loffreda, *Recovering Capharnaum* (Jerusalem: Edizioni Custodia Terra Santa, 1985); and Virgilio Corbo, *The House of Saint Peter at Capharnaum*, trans. Sylvester Saller, Publications of the Studium Biblicum Franciscanum, Collectio minor no. 5 (Jerusalem: Franciscan Printing Press, 1972).

56. Richard A. Batey is convinced that Joseph and Jesus may have helped build the capital at Sepphoris, not far to the west of Nazareth.

See his *Jesus and the Forgotten City: New Light on Sepphoris and the Urban World of Jesus* (Grand Rapids: Baker, 1991).

57. In the fall of 1998 I helped excavate three towers and walls just to the west of the old city of Nazareth. The towers and walls were for agriculture, most likely vineyards. The pottery I found was all Roman, and most was pre-70. Recall not only Isaiah 5 but also, and especially, Mark 12.

58. See the popular booklet by Ehud Netzer entitled *Herodium: An Archaeological Guide* (Jerusalem: Cana, 1987). Also, see Netzer, ed., *Greater Herodium*, Qedem 13 (Jerusalem: Israel Exploration Society, 1981).

59. Yadin's popular account of Masada is at times rather romantic, and he tended to read Josephus's account, which is sometimes fictitious, as if it were a guide to excavations on Masada. See now the definitive studies on Masada: J. Aviram, G. Foerster, and E. Netzer, eds., *Masada: The Yigael Yadin Excavations 1963–1965*, 5 vols. (Jerusalem: Israel Exploration Society, 1989–95).

60. Masterful is Nahman Avigad, *Discovering Jerusalem* (Jerusalem: Shikmona, 1980 [Hebrew]; Nashville: Thomas Nelson, 1983). Invaluable reports and assessments are found in Yigael Yadin, ed., *Jerusalem Revealed: Archaeology in the Holy City 1968–1974* (New Haven and London: Yale University Press, 1976). Essential data regarding the Jerusalem Jesus knew is found in Hillel Geva, ed., *Ancient Jerusalem Revealed* (Jerusalem: Israel Exploration Society, 1994). Dated but authoritative, because it was written by the late Benjamin Mazar, who excavated much of Jerusalem, is *The Mountain of the Lord: Excavating Jerusalem* (Garden City, N.Y.: Doubleday, 1975). A comprehensive assessment of Jerusalem in the eyes of the New Testament authors is Peter W. L. Walker, *Jesus and the Holy City: New Testament Perspectives on Jerusalem* (Grand Rapids: Eerdmans, 1996).

61. The Greek is literally "what stones" (*potapoi lithoi*), but the adjective following these exclamations (*tautas tas megalas oikodomas*) — "these great buildings" — indicates contextually that the stones are massive and not beautiful (contr. RSV [2d ed.]).

62. For the Hebrew and English, see Yigael Yadin, ed., *The Temple Scroll* (Jerusalem: Israel Exploration Society, 1983) 2:222–24.

63. Among the numerous studies on ancient synagogues, see Joseph Gutmann, *Ancient Synagogues: The State of Research*, Brown Judaic Studies 22 (Chico, Calif.: Scholars, 1981); and Lee I. Levine, ed., *Ancient Synagogues Revealed* (Jerusalem: Israel Exploration Society, 1981).

64. See Josephus *Antiquities* 18.2.1; cf. F. Stickert in *Bethsaida*, ed. Rami Arav and Richard A. Freund (Kirksville, Mo.: Thomas Jefferson University Press, 1995) 184.

65. See Josephus *Antiquities* 16.5.1; 17.1.1.

66. See esp. E. Faye and G. Kloetzli, *The Fifth Gospel*, ed. Italo Mancini (Englewood Cliffs, N.J.: Prentice-Hall, 1972); and Bargil Pixner, *With Jesus through Galilee according to the Fifth Gospel* (Collegeville, Minn.: Liturgical Press, 1966).

67. If individuals cannot travel to Israel today, then at least they can study the pictures of the topography; among the many good books, see esp. A. L. Waters and K. A. Marsh with G. M. Burge, *Journey to the Land of Jesus: A Photographic Pilgrimage to the Holy Land* (Lincolnwood, Ill.: Publications International, 1992).

68. I develop this thought in "Intertextuality: Isaiah 40:3 and the Serek Ha-Yahad," in *The Quest for Context and Meaning: Studies in Biblical Intertextuality in Honor of James A. Sanders*, ed. Craig A. Evans and Shemaryahu Talmon (Leiden and New York: Brill, 1997) 197–224.

69. See n. 66.

70. See especially M. A. K. Halliday, *An Introduction to Functional Grammar* (London: Edward Arnold, 1985; 2d ed., 1994); Brian K. Blount, *Cultural Interpretation: Reorienting New Testament Criticism* (Minneapolis: Fortress, 1995). As Blount has shown, "A more comprehensive understanding is approached when an interpreter opens himself or herself to interpretations that originate from beyond the boundaries of his or her own sociolinguistic interpretative background" (p. 90). I wish to stress that interpretations of the New Testament are paradigmatically improved when the exegete and historian live in the land that still speaks a language similar to that used by Jesus.

71. James H. Charlesworth, *The Beloved Disciple* (Valley Forge, Pa.: Trinity Press International, 1995).

72. See Robert W. Funk, *The Acts of Jesus: What Did Jesus Really Do?* (San Francisco: HarperSanFrancisco, 1997).

73. See the following: Charlesworth, *Jesus within Judaism*, 6, 21–22, 167; Craig A. Evans, "Authenticity Criteria in Life of Jesus Research," *Christian Scholars Review* 19 (1989) 6–31; "Authenticity Criteria," *Jesus and His Contemporaries*, Arbeiten zur Geschichte des Antiken Judentums und des Urchristentums 25 (Leiden: Brill, 1995) 13–26; Meier, "Criteria: How Do We Decide What Comes from Jesus?" in *A Marginal Jew*, 167–201; and esp. Gerd Theissen and Dagmar Winter, *Die Kriterienfrage in der Jesusforschung*, Novum Testamentum et Orbis Antiquus 34 (Göttingen: Vandenhoeck and Ruprecht, 1997). For a helpful bibliography on this issue, up to early 1996, see Evans, "Criteria of Authenticity," in *Life of Jesus Research*, 127–46.

74. See James H. Charlesworth and L. L. Johns, eds., *Hillel and Jesus* (Minneapolis: Fortress, 1997).

75. See I. Eph'al and J. Naveh, *Aramaic Ostraca of the Fourth Cen-*

tury BC from Idumaea (Jerusalem: Magnes Press, 1996) 66; see the facing plate.

76. Two works stand out, in my view, as admirable portraits of Jesus' life and teaching. They are Gunther Bornkamm's *Jesus of Nazareth*, trans. Irene McLuskey and Fraser McLuskey with James M. Robinson (New York and London: Harper and Row, 1960); and C. H. Dodd's *The Founder of Christianity* (New York: Collier Books, 1970). It is no accident that both scholars were balanced in their approach and wrote the work near the end of a career characterized by historical erudition and perception. Each knew the sources and requisite methodology.

77. I am convinced that we can use the word "sect" in describing three Jewish groups: the Samaritans, the Essenes (including the Qumranites), and the Palestinian Jesus movement, but we need to jettison the often pejorative overtones of a "sect." See R. Scroggs, "The Earliest Christian Community as Sectarian Movements," *Christianity, Judaism, and Other Greco-Roman Cults,* ed. Jacob Neusner (Leiden: Brill, 1975) 1–23; and B. Wilson, "The Sociology of Sects," *Religion in Sociological Perspective* (Oxford and New York: Oxford University Press, 1982) 89–120.

78. Ben Witherington urges us to contemplate Jesus in light of the Wisdom traditions; see his *Jesus the Sage: The Pilgrimage of Wisdom* (Minneapolis: Fortress, 1994).

79. Still one of the best studies of life in Jerusalem during the time of Jesus is Joachim Jeremias's *Jerusalem during the Time of Jesus: An Investigation into Economic and Social Conditions during the New Testament Period,* trans. F. H. Cave and C. H. Cave (Philadelphia: Fortress, 1967).

80. As Rainer Riesner points out, the messianic authority-motif is a pre-Easter part of Jewish theology. See Riesner, *Jesus als Lehrer,* Wissenschaftliche Untersuchungen zum Neuen Testament 2, Reihe 7, 2d ed. (Tübingen: Mohr [Siebeck], 1984) 352. Also, see Riesner, "Jesus as Preacher and Teacher," in *Jesus and the Oral Gospel Tradition,* ed. Henry Wansbrough, Journal for the Study of the New Testament, Supplement Series 64 (Sheffield: Sheffield Academic Press, 1991) 187–209.

81. For an informed study of Jesus and the revolutionaries of his day, see Richard A. Horsley, *Jesus and the Spiral of Violence: Popular Jewish Resistance in Roman Palestine* (San Francisco: Harper, 1987).

82. See especially two major books on Jesus and politics: Ernst Bammel and C. F. D. Moule, ed., *Jesus and the Politics of His Day* (Cambridge, London, and New York: Cambridge University Press, 1984); and Dovon Mendels, *The Rise and Fall of Jewish Nationalism* (New York and London: Doubleday, 1992); see esp. 209–42. Mendels demonstrates how the concept of kingship changes in the period from 63 B.C.E. to 135 C.E.

83. See esp. Paul Fiebig, *Jüdische Wundergeschichten des neutesta-mentlichen Zeitalters* (Tübingen: Mohr, 1911); and Roman Heiligenthal, *Werke als Zeichen*, Wissenschaftliche Untersuchungen zum Neuen Testament 2, Reihe 9 (Tübingen: Mohr [Siebeck], 1983).

84. See S. Safrai, who rightly states, Jesus "employed educational techniques such as the parable that were common only in Pharisaic teaching." See Safrai, "Jesus and the Hasidim," *Jerusalem Perspective* 42–44 (January–June 1994) 3–22.

85. See esp. the study by F. F. Bruce, *The Hard Sayings of Jesus*, The Jesus Library (London: Hodder and Stoughton, 1983). As Bruce warned, we must not try to make Jesus' hard sayings "easier, for that would be to obscure their meaning" (p. 13).

86. David Flusser with R. Steven Notley, *Jesus*, 2d ed. (Jerusalem: Magnes Press, 1998).

87. See the chapters in James H. Charlesworth, Mark Harding, and Mark Kiley, eds., *The Lord's Prayer and Other Prayer Texts from the Greco-Roman Era* (Valley Forge, Pa.: Trinity Press International, 1994).

88. For further reflections, see Charlesworth, *Jesus within Judaism*, 131–64.

89. Among the many excellent books on the subject of Jesus and women is Ben Witherington's *Women in the Ministry of Jesus*, Society for New Testament Studies, Monograph Series 51 (Cambridge and New York: Cambridge University Press, 1984).

90. For the argument that Jesus was married, see William E. Phipps, *Was Jesus Married?* (New York and London: Harper and Row, 1970) esp. 13–14, 187.

91. For further reflections, see Charlesworth, "Jesus' Concept of God and His Self-Understanding," *Jesus within Judaism*, 131–64.

92. See the similar reflections in Paula Fredriksen, *From Jesus to Christ* (New Haven and London: Yale University Press, 1988) 115.

93. Still vividly memorable are the days I spent with Pierre Benoit in the Old City of Jerusalem. During that time he convinced me that these three terms must refer to Herod's Palace and not to the Antonia Fortress. See Benoit, "Praetorium, Lithostroton, and Gabbatha," *Jesus and the Gospel*, trans. Benet Weatherhead (New York: Seabury, 1973) 1: 167–88.

94. Pinchas Lapide, *The Resurrection of Jesus: A Jewish Perspective*, trans. W. C. Linss (Minneapolis: Augsburg, 1983); David Flusser, *Jesus* (Jerusalem: Magnes Press, 1997) 175–77; and in private conversations. Contrast Bishop Spong's contention that the Resurrection is built on outdated cosmology; Spong, *This Hebrew Lord*, 164–66, 179–81.

95. The reader may find some insights by comparing my list with one published by Sanders in his *Jesus and Judaism*, 326–27.

96. See esp. N. T. Wright's *Jesus and the Victory*.

97. E. P. Sanders, *Jesus and Judaism; Historical Figure of Jesus.*

98. Meier, *A Marginal Jew.*

99. G. Vermes, *Jesus the Jew,* 2d ed. (London: Collins; Philadelphia: Fortress, 1983).

100. Flusser, *Jesus.*

101. Luke T. Johnson, *The Real Jesus: The Misguided Quest for the Historical Jesus and the Truth of the Traditional Gospels* (San Francisco: HarperSanFrancisco, 1996) 177.

102. The counterclaims by Carsten P. Thiede are not persuasive, but see Thiede and Matthew D'Ancona, *Eyewitness to Jesus* (New York: Doubleday, 1996). This book reappeared, with little alteration, as *The Jesus Papyrus* (London: Phoenix, 1997). One of the best rebuttals of Thiede's claims is by Otto Betz and Rainer Riesner; see their "Were Manuscripts of the New Testament Found in Qumran Cave 7?" in *Jesus, Qumran, and the Vatican: Some Clarifications,* trans. John Bowden (New York: Crossroad, 1994) 114–24.

103. Rudolf Bultmann, *Jesus and the Word,* trans. Louise Pettibone Smith and Erminie Huntress Lantero (London and Glasgow: Scribner, 1958 [from the 1934 ed.]) 14.

104. Most of these are discussed in James H. Charlesworth, ed., *Jesus and the Dead Sea Scrolls* (New York: Doubleday, 1992) The Anchor Bible Reference Library.

105. See Marcus J. Borg's moving, but confessional, *Meeting Jesus Again for the First Time: The Historical Jesus and the Heart of Contemporary Faith* (San Francisco: HarperSanFrancisco, 1994, 1995). The Christian and theological content of the book derives from the lectures Borg presented to a conference of the United Church of Christ. For a succinct and sensitive critique of Borg and others in the Jesus Seminar, see L. R. Donelson, "Safe in the Arms of Jesus," *Insights* (spring 1997) 3–13, 47. For a scathing dismissal of the Jesus Seminar, see Luke T. Johnson, *The Real Jesus.*

106. See the same point made by Jaroslav Pelikan in his *Jesus through the Centuries* (New Haven and London: Yale University Press, 1985) 10.

107. See the chapters in Charlesworth and Johns, *Hillel and Jesus.*

108. I know this not from reading books but talking to Roman Catholics who are disillusioned about the church's failure to teach them what might be known, historically and sociologically, about Jesus.

109. *"The message of Jesus* is a presupposition for the theology of the New Testament rather than a part of that theology itself." Rudolf Bultmann, *Theology of the New Testament,* trans. Kendrick Grobel (New York: Scribner, 1951) 1:3. For the most recent German original, see *Theologie des Neuen Testaments,* 9th ed. reworked by Otto Merk (Tübingen: Mohr

[Siebeck], 1984) 1. The German literally means: "The proclamation of Jesus belongs to the presuppositions of New Testament theology and is not a part of it itself."

110. Leonhard Goppelt showed conclusively that "the root [Wurzel] of New Testament theology" is the Easter kerygma, but its "base (actually "groundwork" to avoid a mixed metaphor [German: Grundlage])" is "the recounting of the ministry of Jesus." Goppelt, *Theology of the New Testament*, trans. John Alsup (Grand Rapids: Eerdmans, 1981) 1:7. For the German, see Goppelt, *Theologie des Neuen Testaments*, 3d ed., ed. Jurgen Roloff (Göttingen: Vandenhoeck and Ruprecht, 1975) 58.

111. See James H. Charlesworth, "The Date of the Parables of Enoch (1 En 37–71)," *Henoch* 20 (1998) 93–98.

112. As A. E. Harvey stated, "Archaeology has tended in recent years to enhance the credibility of the gospel narratives." See his important *Jesus and the Constraints of History* (Philadelphia: Westminster, 1982) 3. I am impressed how much more obvious this claim is today than when it was made over seventeen years ago.

Index